More Picture Stories

Language and Problem-Posing Activities for Beginners

More Picture Stories

Language and Problem-Posing Activities for Beginners

FRED LIGON
ELIZABETH TANNENBAUM
CAROL RICHARDSON RODGERS
In Association with The Experiment in International Living

Illustrations by Fred Ligon

More Picture Stories: Language and Problem-Posing Activities for Beginners

Longman, 10 Bank Street, White Plains, NY 10606

Associated companies:
Longman Group Ltd., London
Longman Cheshire Pty., Melbourne
Longman Paul Pty., Auckland
Copp Clark Pitman, Toronto

Distributed in the United Kingdom by Longman Group
Ltd., Longman House, Burnt Mill, Harlow, Essex CM20
2JE, England, and by associated companies, branches,
and representatives throughout the world.

Executive editor: Joanne Dresner
Development editor: Debbie Sistino
Production editor: Andrea West
Cover design: Suzanne Lobel
Cover illustration: Fred Ligon
Text art: Fred Ligon
Production supervisor: Richard Bretan

Library of Congress Cataloging-in-Publication Data

Ligon, Fred.
    More picture stories : language and problem posing activities /
Fred Ligon, Elizabeth Tannenbaum, Carol Richardson Rodgers, in
association with the Experiment in International Living.
        p.   cm.
    ISBN 0-8013-0839-9
    1. English language—Textbooks for foreign speakers.
I. Tannenbaum, Elizabeth.   II. Rodgers, Carol Richardson.
III. Experiment in International Living.   IV. Rodgers, Carol
Richardson.   V. Title.
PE1128.L4636   1992
428.2′4—dc20   91-38098
                                                              CIP

7 8 9 10-CRS-99 98

Contents

Introduction

More Picture Stories: Language and Problem-Posing Activities for Beginners consists of 16 picture stories for adult and young adult ESL students who have limited English ability and limited familiarity with U.S. cultural practices. The stories are appropriate for students with basic literacy skills and with survival ESL needs as well as for higher level students who are beginning to use their language to deal with everyday problems at work and at home.

Told through a sequence of 10 pictures, each story deals with a particular cultural topic. The topics are presented through situations and everyday events that might happen to newcomers adjusting to life in the U.S. The characters in the stories know very little English, have minimal literacy skills and have little knowledge of American culture. The experiences of the characters allow students to analyze their own situations, evaluate options and anticipate potential problems before they happen as well as to explore alternative ways of dealing with existing problems in their own lives. The humor in the stories makes them fun to read and encourages discussion and debate.

The book consists of two parts: 16 student units and a Teacher's Notes section with separate notes for each student unit. Before beginning to work with the units:

- Look through the Table of Contents and Topic Chart. Read the story titles.
- Choose a story based on the needs or interests of the class.
- Look through the exercises in the chosen story.
- Read through the Teacher's Notes for that story at the back of the book.

STUDENT UNIT EXERCISES

All student units follow the same format and include exercises for listening, speaking, reading, and writing. All units also include a series of questions which encourage critical thinking about a particular problem. No unit is dependent on any other, so you may select any unit related to a chosen topic. However, all the stories take place in the same town. By using the map on the inside front cover of the book and finding the location of each story, students can think of the characters as part of one community.

The exercises can be used with a variety of current ESL methodologies. Exercises include options for work with the whole class, small groups, pairs or individuals. The variety of exercises also addresses various learning styles and includes teacher-directed as well as student-directed exercises.

Talk about the Pictures.

A series of pictures, which read from left to right and from top to bottom (just as the pages of a book are read), provides the stimulus for oral language. These pictures establish a context for the literacy work to be done later by giving students the oral vocabulary and the needed cultural background information to understand the text. They create a motivation for reading because of student interest and involvement in the stories.

Procedure: Students look at the pictures and describe them. Students may be able to produce only a single word description. Accept several students' responses, and then create a clear statement. For example (Unit 1, 12 Hours Old):

TEACHER:	What do you see in Frame 1?
STUDENT 1:	Woman
STUDENT 2:	Girl
STUDENT 3:	Cooking dinner
TEACHER:	Right. The woman is cooking dinner for her daughter.

As students generate vocabulary and possibly sentences for each frame, write their words on the board. Exposure to the written language now will help students connect print to oral language and prepare them for the literacy exercises in the rest of the unit.

After the students have generated language for each frame, they are ready to listen to the entire story. Tell the story, expanding on the vocabulary generated by the students, or have the class tell the story together, incorporating previously generated vocabulary. A number of different types of questions can be used to guide the telling of the story:

- Description: What do you see in Frame 1? What's the woman doing?
- Sequence: What did the man do first? Then what did he do? What happened after that?
- Speculation: Do you think the man can read? Do you think he saw the sign?
- Prediction: What do you think will happen in Frame 7? What will happen after Frame 10?

The story can be told several times with teacher and students working together to refine the language. After adequate oral practice with the whole group, have students work in pairs to describe each frame. At this point accuracy is not essential. Note: Although sample language for each frame is given in the Teacher's Notes, students should be encouraged to produce their own language.

Expansion Exercises

Grammar: Included in the Teacher's Notes is a list of possible grammar points to cover for each story. It should be noted that all units can be used for verb practice as well as other grammatical points. The grammar points listed for each story are ones that the story seems to lend itself to.

Discussion: It is appropriate to present this section (on the last page of each unit) during Exercise A. The procedure for using these questions is explained under the *What Do You Think*? section of this introduction.

Comprehension: After the story has been told, check student comprehension by giving commands which require only nonverbal responses, for example, "Point to the woman. Put an X on the stove. Circle the pan."

Frame by Frame: Make a copy of the story and cut it into frames. Before students see the story in the book, give groups of students one frame at a time. After handing out each frame, ask, "What is happening? What do you think will happen next?"

Action Sequence: Many of the stories include a sequence of steps that lead to a specific end result. Some examples are: packing a suitcase, following a recipe, making toast. Using pictures or props, present the language to describe the steps in the activity. For example, demonstrate putting bread in a toaster. Have students follow your directions and then give each other the commands.

Role-Play: Each story can be acted out by the students in role-play form. Students can either mime the parts while the teacher (or another student) reads the text, or they can actually playact the story. In both cases, using props and creatively setting a stage can encourage student participation.

Number the Pictures in Order. Then Tell the Story.

This exercise focuses on sequencing skills and on the concept that stories have a beginning, a middle, and an end.

Procedure: Point out that Frame 1 has already been numbered. Have students work individually or in pairs to number the rest of the pictures in order. Check the answers by reading aloud the numbers from top to bottom in each column, by having individual students read aloud the numbers, or by having students in pairs or small groups compare their answers. Then have the whole class, small groups, or pairs tell the story.

Variations

Scrambled Pictures: Make copies of the picture story and cut them into frames. Give each group of students a cut-up picture story to put in order.

Narration: Narrate the story and have students number the frames in the order read. This variation works especially well with stories that have a possibility of more than one correct order.

Match the Picture with the Sentence.

This exercise focuses on connecting oral language to written language: both the previously practiced oral language as well as the student-generated language that the teacher has written on the board.

Procedure: First do the example sentence with the whole class. Then have students draw a line from the picture frame to the sentence that relates to that frame. Prepare less literate classes for this exercise by writing sentences before asking students to work on their own. Have students check their work in pairs or by having individual students read aloud the print that matches each of the frames.

Variation

Matching Pairs: Write one sentence (or key word) for each frame on a 3x5 card. Cut up the picture story and paste each frame on a card. Have students match each picture frame with the appropriate sentence (or key word). Divide the class into pairs or small groups. Give each a set of the cards and have the students place the cards in scrambled order face down on a table. Have students take turns turning over two cards at a time to find a match. As the students turn over the cards, they can orally describe the picture or read aloud the sentence. The student with the most matches is the winner.

Listen to the Teacher.

The listening exercises focus on real communication situations such as understanding addresses, phone numbers, or prices. In some activities, students are asked to pick out one piece of information from a conversation which will encourage students to focus on listening for specific information.

Procedure: Teach the vocabulary in the exercise by following the suggestions in the Teacher's Notes for each unit. Read aloud the script from the Teacher's Notes section. Do number one with the whole class. Show students how to indicate (circle, write, number) the correct answer. Then have them listen and complete the exercise. Have students check their answers on the board, or by taking the role of the teacher and reading the answers to the class.

Expansion Exercise

Change the Script: After doing the exercise once using the script, change the script, for example: read item c instead of item a, and do the activity again in order to practice with different vocabulary. The script can also be made easier or more difficult depending on the level of the class.

Play the Game.

The games put the language into real-life situations. They shift the focus away from the teacher and help students learn from each other. They encourage cooperation and help students develop the skill of completing a task on their own.

Procedure: First teach the relevant vocabulary on the page. Ask students to circle any words they don't know. Then have students work in pairs or small groups to decide the meaning of any new words by matching each of the words with one of the frames from the picture story. For words not used in the picture story, make classroom visuals that illustrate the word and have students match the visual to the word card. For common sight words (such as No Smoking, Emergency Room, Don't Walk), make large word cards and post them around the room so students will constantly be exposed to them. Have students explain where they might see these words outside of class. Next draw the game on the board. Ask two students to come to the front of the room. Demonstrate the game rules written in the student text at the beginning of each game. Have the two students follow your directions. Be sure to point out start, finish, the direction of the play, and where to write the answers. Finally, divide students into pairs and give each pair the materials needed to play the game.

- Markers: Use items such as bingo chips, small pieces of paper, or bottle caps. Each pair needs two markers of different colors (shapes or sizes) for the board games and two different color sets of five markers for Three-In-A-Row.
- Dice: Provide each pair of students with one die.

Circle T for True or F for False.

Students use their knowledge of the story and their developing reading comprehension skills to draw conclusions. All the words and sentence structures in this exercise have been seen previously. In this exercise students encounter the familiar words and structures in new arrangements.

Procedure: Write the first statement on the board with T F by it. Read it to the class and ask students if the statement is true or false. Show students how to indicate the correct answer. Then have students read and complete the exercise. After they have finished, have students check their work in small groups or as a class by having individual students read the sentences aloud and tell if the statement is true or false.

Expansion Exercise

Rewriting: Students rewrite the false statements to make them true.

Fill in the Blanks.

This exercise gives students the opportunity to write what they have already seen in print in the previous exercises.

Procedure: Do the first blank together as a class. Then have students work individually or in pairs to fill in the remaining blanks with an appropriate word. Initially students may need to copy words from other places in the text or work together to write the words.

Variations

Copying: For less literate students, write the words that are used to fill in the blanks on the board in random order. Have students choose the appropriate word for each blank and copy it in the appropriate place.

Dictation: Read the Fill-in-the-Blanks passage aloud; have students fill in the blanks with the words they hear.

Grammar Focus: Write the Fill-in-the-Blanks passage on the board, leaving blanks for different parts of speech such as verbs or pronouns.

What do you think?

Students refer to the picture story in Exercise A and explore a series of related questions. The first questions assess the students' comprehension of the story. Since the facts of many of the stories are open to interpretation, there is not always just one correct answer to the comprehension questions. Subsequent questions ask students to relate the story to their own experience, using the story as a way of examining the circumstances of their own lives. Rather than offering any right solutions to students, you should encourage students to generate and explore a number of possible paths of action. Any solutions should come from the students themselves.

Procedure: Ask information questions and make sure students have comprehended the story. Ask students to relate the story to their own experiences. This might be done in small groups to create an atmosphere more conducive to personal discussion and sharing. Have students generate possible courses of action for both the character in the story and, if appropriate, their own lives.

Write the Story.

This final exercise in each of the units is a culmination of the work in the previous exercises. It reinforces the previous work with vocabulary, sentence word order, syntax, and sequencing. For the first time, students write complete sentences in a narrative form. However, the focus is on expressing ideas and not on grammatical accuracy.

Procedure: Key Words. Have students work with a partner (or with the entire class) to write key words that they remember from the story. Assist students in writing words they cannot spell.

Write the Story. Have students use the key words they have identified and the first and last picture frames to cue their writing of the story. Work with individual students, asking clarification questions and helping the students spell words they are having trouble putting into print. Do not demand perfect grammar or a sentence for each frame. Some students will initially be able to write only a few words or partial sentences.

Expansion Excercises

Student-to-Student Reading: Have students read their writing to each other. Then have them rewrite their stories with any changes they might want to make.

Student-to-Student Editing: Have students read each other's writing and make editing suggestions.

Class Composition: Have students contribute sentences from their own stories, working together to create a class composition.

Class Editing: Choose sentences with common errors from several students' compositions. Write these sentences anonymously on the board and have the class work together to do the editing.

TEACHER'S NOTES

Following the student text are detailed notes to the teacher for each unit. These notes provide:

1. Background information (topic, functions, situation, cultural notes, grammar focus).
2. Procedures for setting up each exercise and answer keys.
3. Suggestions for variations and expansion exercises.

GUIDING PRINCIPLES

We have based our writing of each chapter on several guiding principles. First, in designing the reading and writing activities, we drew on the principles of whole language and process writing. We also were guided by the belief that students should be empowered to make sense of and have control over their lives. By being taught to think critically through a series of problems posed by each story, students can begin this process. Finally, we believe that learning and change happen not in isolation, but within a community, and have designed activities which foster the necessary skills and awarenesses to work effectively with others.

Topic Chart

TOPICS		Unit 1 12 Hours Old	Unit 2 At the Supermarket	Unit 3 D3 to E4	Unit 4 The Dentist	Unit 5 Do Not Touch	Unit 6 The Heater	Unit 7 House on Fire	Unit 8 The Job Interview	Unit 9 No Exit	Unit 10 OK, No Job	Unit 11 One Hour	Unit 12 Packing	Unit 13 Pancakes	Unit 14 Stay for Dinner	Unit 15 The Toaster	Unit 16 The Wallet
CLOTHING:	Appropriate Dress										●		●		●		
	Clothing Items														●		●
EMPLOYMENT:	Employer-Employee Relations			●							●		●	●			
	Finding a Job										●						
	Legal Rights										●		●				
	Male-Female Roles			●							●		●				
	On-the-Job Responsibilities			●		●							●	●			
	Sexual Harassment												●				
FOOD:	Comparison Shopping		●														
	Following a Recipe													●			
	Food Items		●											●		●	
	Food Storage	●														●	
HEALTH:	Costs/Insurance	●			●							●					
	The Dentist				●												
	Emergencies	●		●	●			●		●		●					
	Food Storage	●															
	Illness/Accident Prevention	●	●			●	●					●				●	
HOUSING:	Emergencies							●		●							
	Safety							●		●							
	Tenants' Rights							●		●							
LAW AND ORDER:	Responsibilities/Rights										●	●	●				●
LIFESTYLES:	Dating													●	●		
	Male-Female Relationships										●		●	●	●		
	Male-Female Roles			●							●		●				
	Parent-Child Relationships														●		
	Values		●				●			●			●	●	●	●	●
SAFETY:	Emergencies	●		●			●	●	●	●		●				●	
	Safety in the City											●					●
	Safety in the Home	●						●		●						●	
	Safety in the Workplace			●			●		●								
TELEPHONE:	911/Emergencies	●		●			●	●	●	●		●				●	
	Making Appointments				●						●						
TRANSPORTATION:	Safety											●					
	Traffic/Pedestrian Rules/Signs											●					
WEATHER:	Appropriate Clothing							●						●			
	Climate							●									

xi

More Picture Stories

Language and Problem-Posing Activities for Beginners

12 Hours Old

A. Talk about the pictures.

NOTE: Discussion questions appear in Exercise G.

B. Number the pictures in order. Then tell the story.

C. Match the picture with the sentence.

1.

2.

3.

4.

5.

6.

7.

a. The woman cooks dinner at 7:00 p.m.

b. The daughter wakes up at 6:30 a.m.

c. The daughter wants to watch TV.

d. The daughter has a stomachache.

e. The woman takes the pan of meat to the table.

f. The woman takes her daughter to the emergency room.

g. The woman and her daughter eat dinner at 8:00 p.m.

D. Where do you put it?

1.  _d_

2.  _____

3.  _____

4. 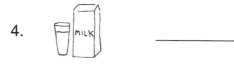 _____

5.  _____

6. _____

7.  _____

8.  _____

9.  _____

10.  _____

a.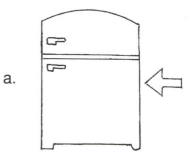

b.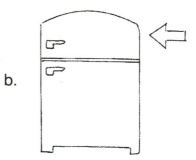

c.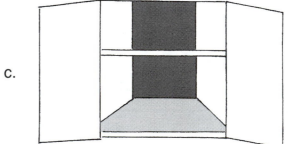

d.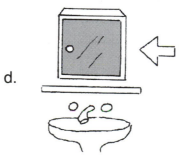

4   Unit 1

E. Circle T for True or F for False.

1. The woman takes her daughter to school. T F

2. The daughter wants to watch TV. T F

3. The woman and her daughter eat dinner at 8:00 p.m. T F

4. The food is on the stove for 15 hours. T F

5. The daughter eats again at 5:00 a.m. T F

6. The woman cooks breakfast at 7:00 a.m. T F

7. The daughter has a stomachache. T F

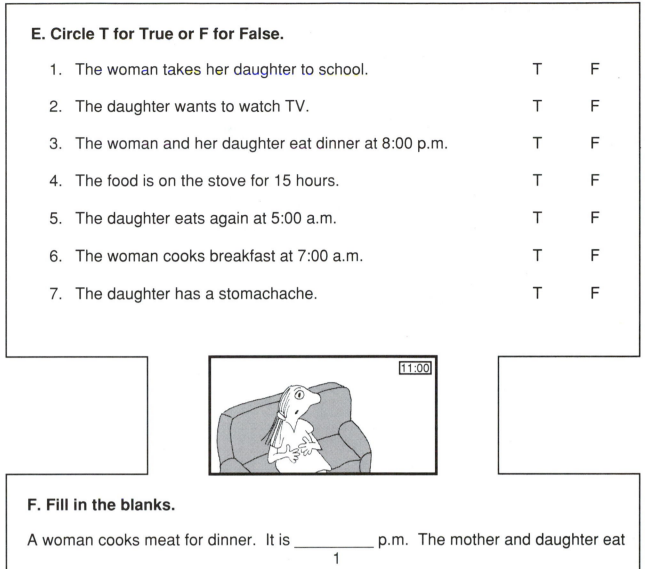

F. Fill in the blanks.

A woman cooks meat for dinner. It is _____ p.m. The mother and daughter eat
    1

_____ at 8:00 p.m. The _____ wants to watch TV.
    2   3

The woman tells her daughter to go to _____. The pan of meat
                                            4

is on the _____ for 12 _____. The _____ wakes up
            5   6   7

at 6:30 a.m. She goes to the kitchen. Her mother _____ the pan of meat
                                                        8

to the table. Her daughter eats the meat. She has a _____.
                                                          9

The woman takes her daughter to the _____ room.
                                          10

G. What do you think? Look at Exercise A. Answer these questions.

What happens to the girl? Why does she get sick? Where do the girl and her mother go for help? Did you ever go to the emergency room? What was it like? How much does it cost to go to the emergency room? Did the girl need to go to the emergency room?

H. Work with your teacher or a partner. Write words you remember from the story.

_____

Now write the story. Use the words to help you.

At the Supermarket

A. Talk about the pictures.

NOTE: Discussion questions appear in Exercise H.

B. Number the pictures in order. Then tell the story.

C. Match the picture with the sentence.

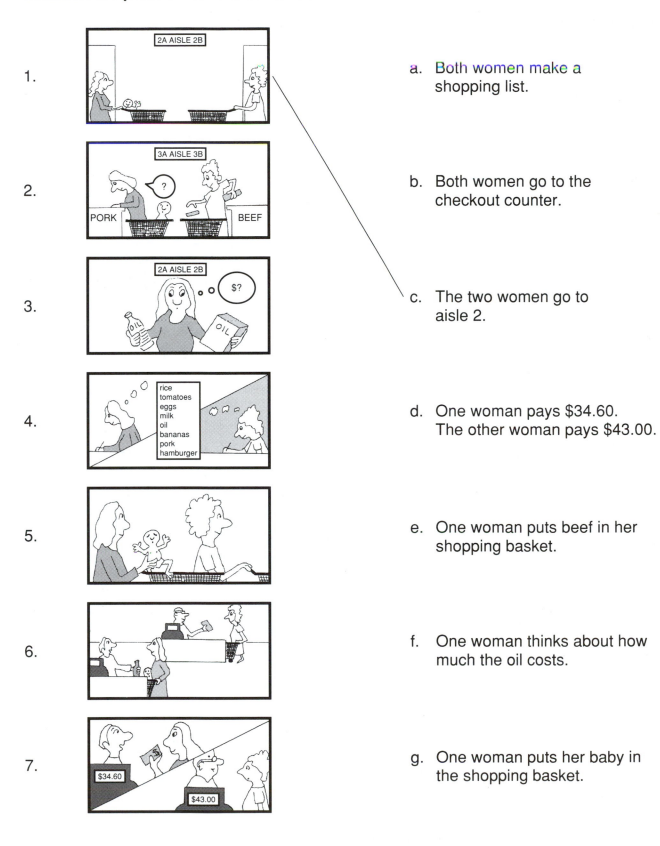

1.

2.

3.

4.

5.

6.

7.

a. Both women make a shopping list.

b. Both women go to the checkout counter.

c. The two women go to aisle 2.

d. One woman pays $34.60. The other woman pays $43.00.

e. One woman puts beef in her shopping basket.

f. One woman thinks about how much the oil costs.

g. One woman puts her baby in the shopping basket.

D. Listen to the teacher. Circle the price you hear.

1.	a. 99¢	b. 89¢	c. 98¢
2.	a. $1.03	b. $13.01	c. $3.01
3.	a. $1.98	b. $1.89	c. $1.19
4.	a. 49¢	b. 41¢	c. 14¢
5.	a. $2.18	b. $2.80	c. $2.08
6.	a. $43.00	b. $4.30	c. $3.40
7.	a. 54¢	b. $1.54	c. 51¢

E. Look at the food in each row. Which one would you buy? Why? Circle the letter.

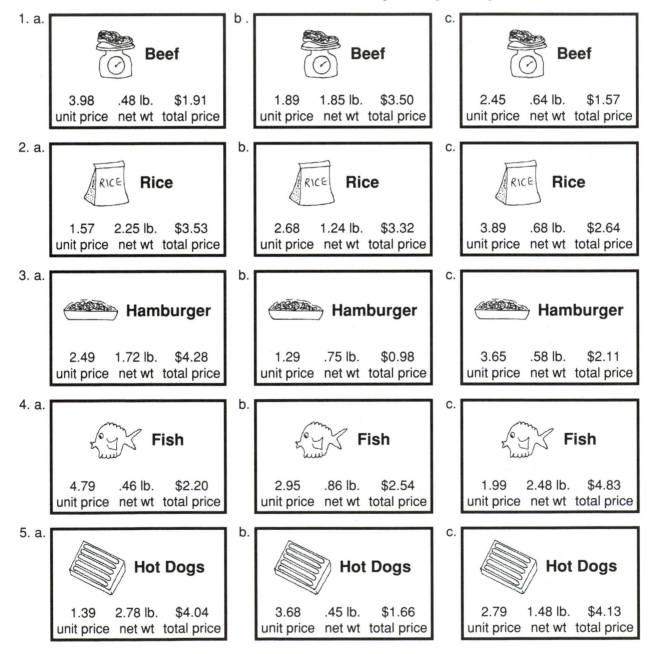

1. a. **Beef**
   3.98   .48 lb. $1.91
   unit price net wt total price

   b. **Beef**
   1.89   1.85 lb. $3.50
   unit price net wt total price

   c. **Beef**
   2.45   .64 lb. $1.57
   unit price net wt total price

2. a. **Rice**
   1.57   2.25 lb. $3.53
   unit price net wt total price

   b. **Rice**
   2.68   1.24 lb. $3.32
   unit price net wt total price

   c. **Rice**
   3.89   .68 lb. $2.64
   unit price net wt total price

3. a. **Hamburger**
   2.49   1.72 lb. $4.28
   unit price net wt total price

   b. **Hamburger**
   1.29   .75 lb. $0.98
   unit price net wt total price

   c. **Hamburger**
   3.65   .58 lb. $2.11
   unit price net wt total price

4. a. **Fish**
   4.79   .46 lb. $2.20
   unit price net wt total price

   b. **Fish**
   2.95   .86 lb. $2.54
   unit price net wt total price

   c. **Fish**
   1.99   2.48 lb. $4.83
   unit price net wt total price

5. a. **Hot Dogs**
   1.39   2.78 lb. $4.04
   unit price net wt total price

   b. **Hot Dogs**
   3.68   .45 lb. $1.66
   unit price net wt total price

   c. **Hot Dogs**
   2.79   1.48 lb. $4.13
   unit price net wt total price

F. Circle T for True or F for False.

1. One woman buys apples.   T   F

2. One woman brings her baby to the supermarket.   T   F

3. Both women want to buy milk.   T   F

4. Three women go to the supermarket.   T   F

5. One woman thinks about how much the oil costs.   T   F

6. Both women go to the checkout counter.   T   F

7. Both women pay $43.00.   T   F

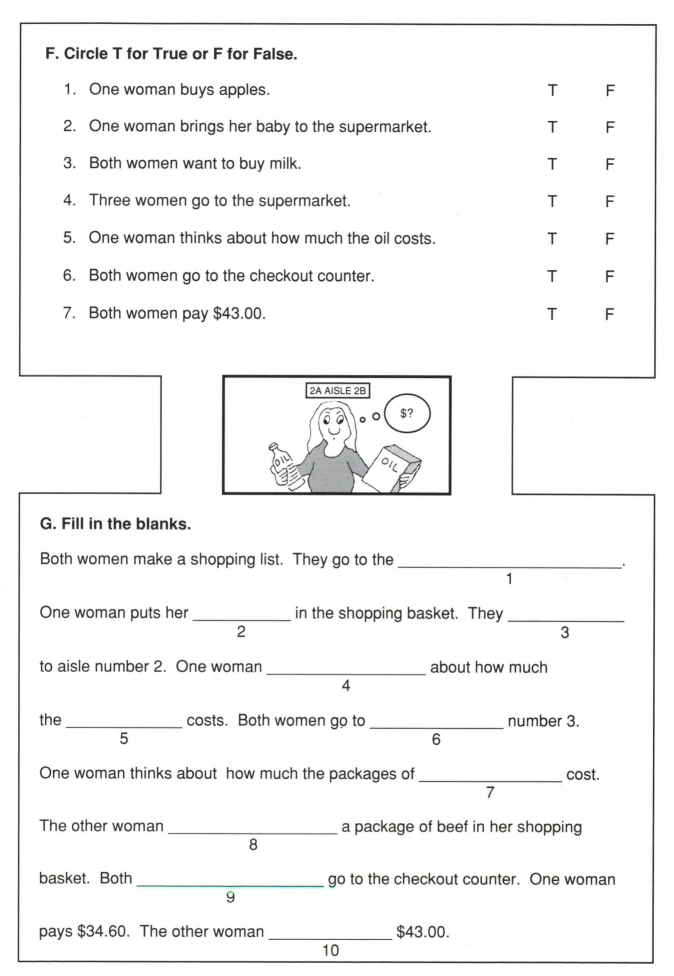

G. Fill in the blanks.

Both women make a shopping list. They go to the _____.
                                                                                            1

One woman puts her _____ in the shopping basket. They _____
                                          2   3

to aisle number 2. One woman _____ about how much
                                                             4

the _____ costs. Both women go to _____ number 3.
             5   6

One woman thinks about how much the packages of _____ cost.
                                                                                        7

The other woman _____ a package of beef in her shopping
                                           8

basket. Both _____ go to the checkout counter. One woman
                              9

pays $34.60. The other woman _____ $43.00.
                                                      10

H. What do you think? Look at Exercise A. Answer these questions.

What are the two women doing? How does the first woman shop? How does the second woman shop? When you go to the supermarket, how do you decide what to buy? What can the second woman do to save money?

I. Work with your teacher or a partner. Write words you remember from the story.

_____

_____

Now write the story. Use the words to help you.

rice
tomatoes
eggs
milk
oil
bananas
pork
hamburger

$34.60

$43.00

A. Talk about the pictures.

NOTE: Discussion questions appear in Exercise H.

B. Number the pictures in order. Then tell the story.

14   Unit 3

C. Match the picture with the sentence.

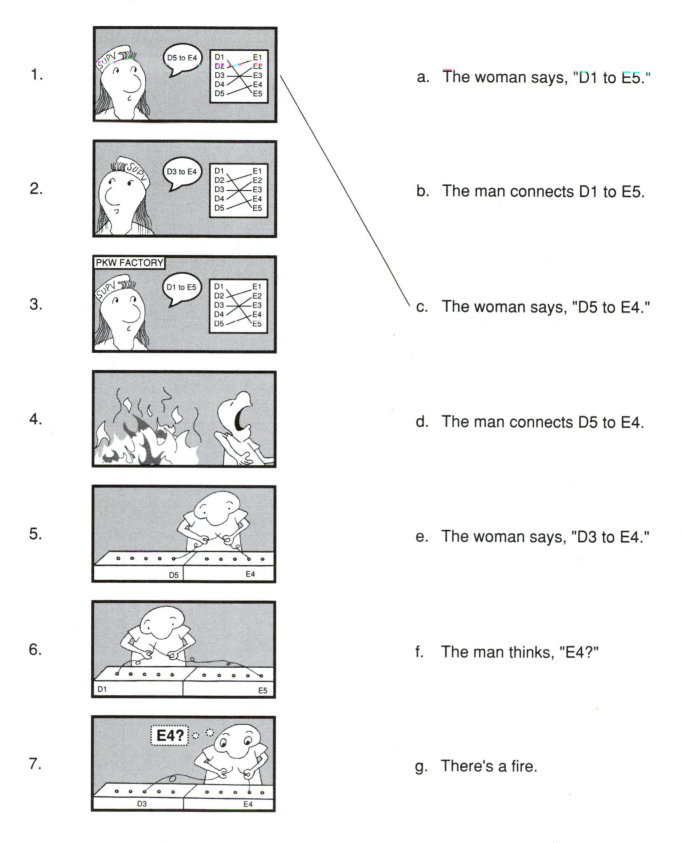

1.

a. The woman says, "D1 to E5."

2.

b. The man connects D1 to E5.

3.

c. The woman says, "D5 to E4."

4.

d. The man connects D5 to E4.

5.

e. The woman says, "D3 to E4."

6.

f. The man thinks, "E4?"

7.

g. There's a fire.

D. Listen to the teacher. Draw a line.

1.
D1	E3
D2	E4
D3	E5
D4	E6

(a line drawn from D1 to E5)

2.
B3	G3
B4	G4
B5	G5
B6	G6

3.
A2	C4
A3	C5
A4	C6
A5	C7

4.
E1	F6
E2	F7
E3	F8
E4	F9

5.
C3	J3
C4	J4
C5	J5
C6	J6

6.
F6	K8
F7	K9
F8	K10
F9	K11

E. Look at the words and the map. Find the buildings. Write the letter and the number under each word.

1. supermarket
   C 4

2. bookstore
   ___ ___

3. hospital
   ___ ___

4. drugstore
   ___ ___

5. coffee shop
   ___ ___

6. bank
   ___ ___

7. bus station
   ___ ___

8. clinic
   ___ ___

9. school
   ___ ___

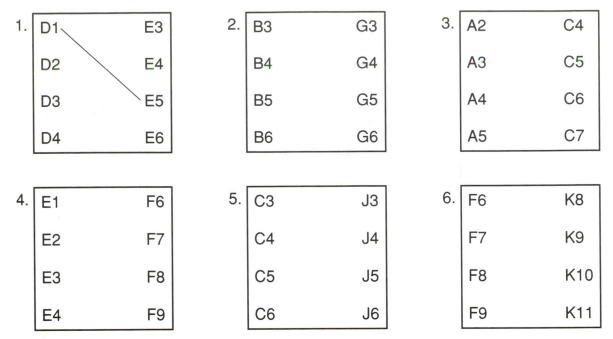

F. Circle T for True or F for False.

1. The man listens to the directions.   T   F

2. The woman reads the letters and numbers.   T   F

3. The man puts the wires together.   T   F

4. The man connects D3 to E4.   T   F

5. The man is the supervisor.   T   F

6. The woman connects D3 to E4.   T   F

7. The man tells the supervisor, "There's a problem." T   F

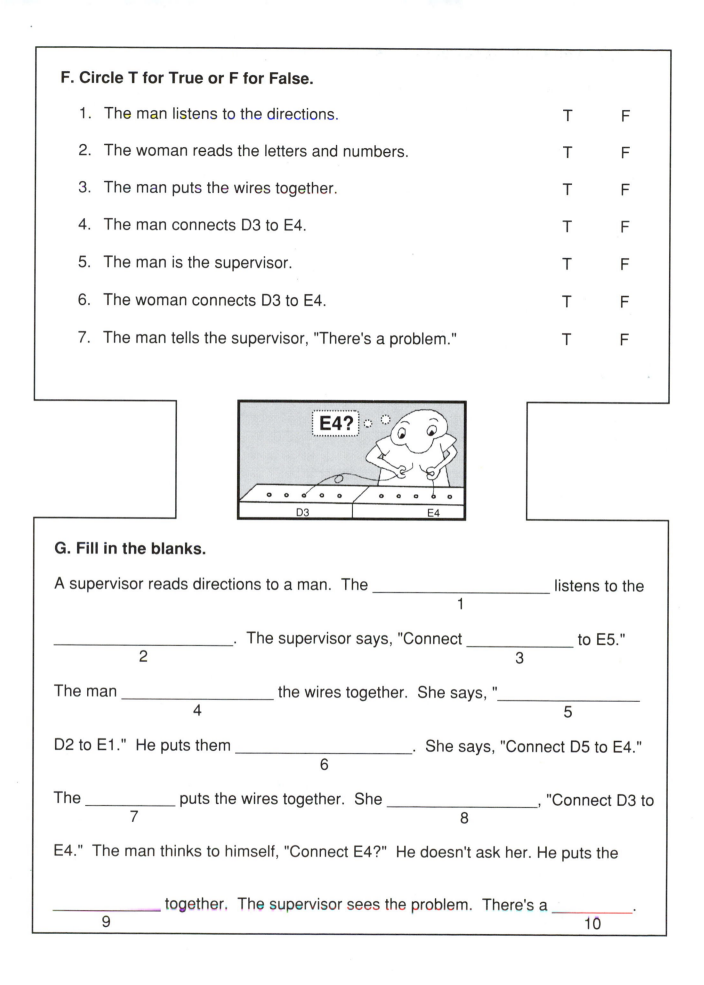

G. Fill in the blanks.

A supervisor reads directions to a man. The _____ listens to the
                                                    1

_____. The supervisor says, "Connect _____ to E5."
        2   3

The man _____ the wires together. She says, "_____
                4   5

D2 to E1." He puts them _____. She says, "Connect D5 to E4."
                                6

The _____ puts the wires together. She _____, "Connect D3 to
          7   8

E4." The man thinks to himself, "Connect E4?" He doesn't ask her. He puts the

_____ together. The supervisor sees the problem. There's a _____.
   9   10

H. What do you think? Look at Exercise A. Answer these questions.

Who is the boss, the man or the woman? What is the man doing? What is the woman doing? Why is there a fire? Why didn't the man correct the woman? Did you ever refuse to do something at work? Why? What happened? What should the man do?

I. Work with your teacher or a partner. Write words you remember from the story.

_____

Now write the story. Use the words to help you.

The Dentist

A. Talk about the pictures.

NOTE: Discussion questions appear in Exercise G.

B. Number the pictures in order. Then tell the story.

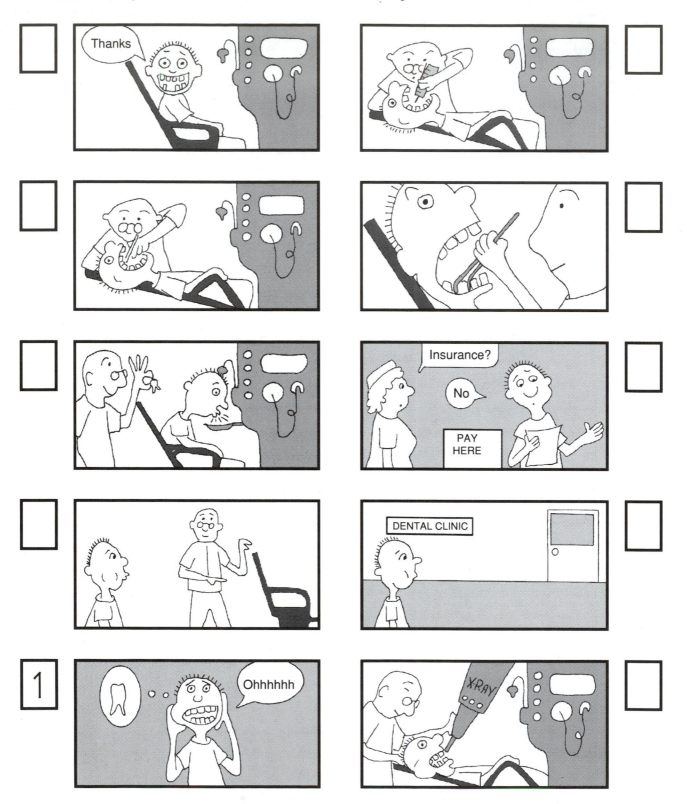

C. Match the picture with the sentence.

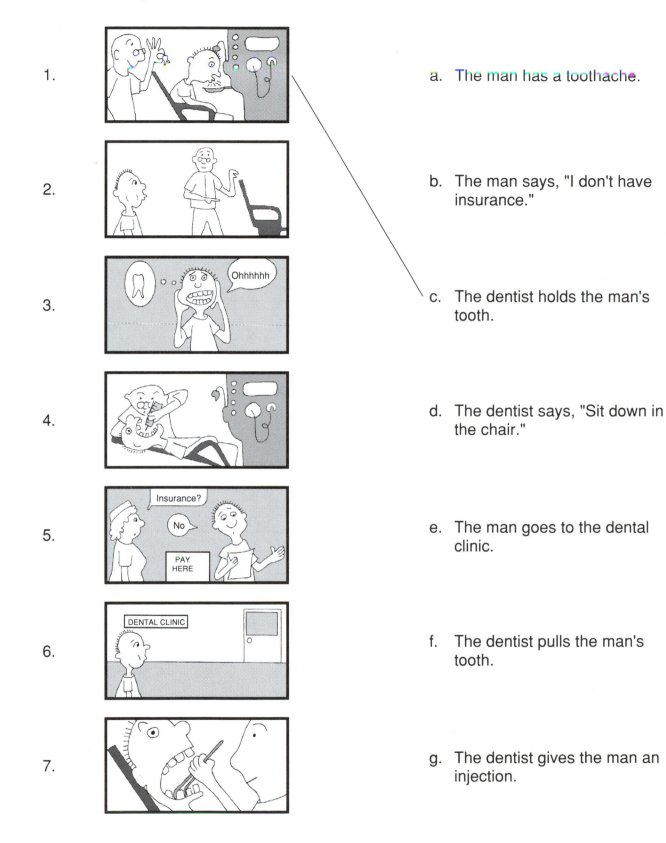

1.

2.

3.

4.

5.

6.

7.

a. The man has a toothache.

b. The man says, "I don't have insurance."

c. The dentist holds the man's tooth.

d. The dentist says, "Sit down in the chair."

e. The man goes to the dental clinic.

f. The dentist pulls the man's tooth.

g. The dentist gives the man an injection.

**D. Listen to the teacher. Write the words you hear on appointment card 1.
Repeat with cards 2-6.**

(1)

> **JILL M. SMITH, D.D.S.**
> 4 California St.
> Phone 555-7328
>
> Mr. E. Lee
> has an appointment on
>
> Day   Month   Date
>
> At   A.M.   P.M.
>
> Please telephone one day in advance if you
> will be unable to keep the appointment.

(2)

> **JILL M. SMITH, D.D.S.**
> 4 California St.
> Phone 555-7328
>
> Mrs. B. Brown
> has an appointment on
>
> Day   Month   Date
>
> At   A.M.   P.M.
>
> Please telephone one day in advance if you
> will be unable to keep the appointment.

(3)

> **JILL M. SMITH, D.D.S.**
> 4 California St.
> Phone 555-7328
>
> Mr. P. Brown
> has an appointment on
>
> Day   Month   Date
>
> At   A.M.   P.M.
>
> Please telephone one day in advance if you
> will be unable to keep the appointment.

(4)

> **JILL M. SMITH, D.D.S.**
> 4 California St.
> Phone 555-7328
>
> Ms. K. Lee
> has an appointment on
>
> Day   Month   Date
>
> At   A.M.   P.M.
>
> Please telephone one day in advance if you
> will be unable to keep the appointment.

(5)

> **JILL M. SMITH, D.D.S.**
> 4 California St.
> Phone 555-7328
>
> Mr. G. Rice
> has an appointment on
>
> Day   Month   Date
>
> At   A.M.   P.M.
>
> Please telephone one day in advance if you
> will be unable to keep the appointment.

(6)

> **JILL M. SMITH, D.D.S.**
> 4 California St.
> Phone 555-7328
>
> Ms. N. Rice
> has an appointment on
>
> Day   Month   Date
>
> At   A.M.   P.M.
>
> Please telephone one day in advance if you
> will be unable to keep the appointment.

E. Circle T for True or F for False.

1. The dentist pulls the man's tooth.   T   F

2. The dentist spits in the sink.   T   F

3. The dentist has a toothache.   T   F

4. The woman says, "Sit down in the chair."   T   F

5. The dentist looks in the man's mouth.   T   F

6. The dentist takes an x-ray.   T   F

7. The man goes to the dental clinic.   T   F

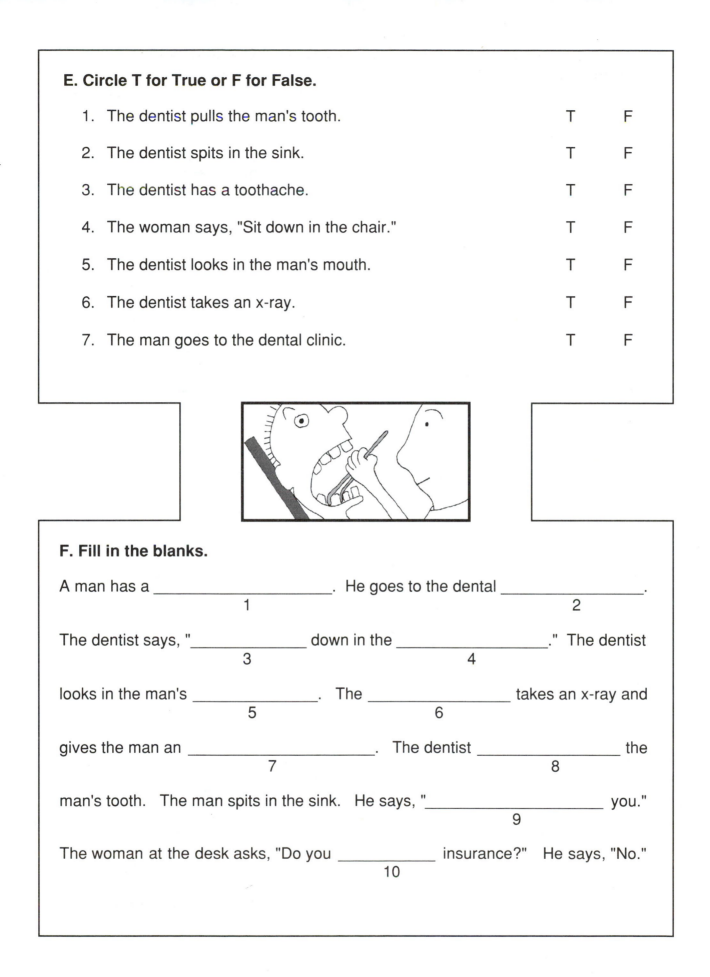

F. Fill in the blanks.

A man has a _____. He goes to the dental _____.
                          1   2

The dentist says, "_____ down in the _____." The dentist
                              3   4

looks in the man's _____. The _____ takes an x-ray and
                              5   6

gives the man an _____. The dentist _____ the
                              7   8

man's tooth. The man spits in the sink. He says, "_____ you."
                                                                    9

The woman at the desk asks, "Do you _____ insurance?" He says, "No."
                                                  10

G. What do you think? Look at Exercise A. Answer these questions.

What is the man's problem? What does the dentist do? Did you ever have a toothache? What did you do? How can you prevent a toothache? How much does it cost for a dentist to pull a tooth? How can the man pay if he does not have insurance?

H. Work with your teacher or a partner. Write words you remember from the story.

_____

Now write the story. Use the words to help you.

Do Not Touch

A. Talk about the pictures.

NOTE: Discussion questions appear in Exercise H.

B. Number the pictures in order. Then tell the story.

C. Match the picture with the sentence.

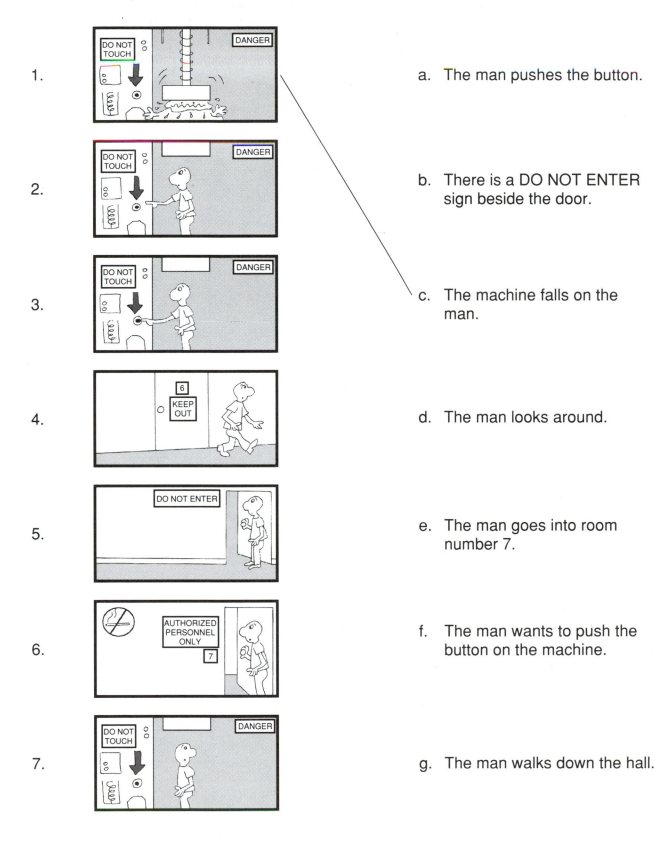

1.

2.

3.

4.

5.

6.

7.

a. The man pushes the button.

b. There is a DO NOT ENTER sign beside the door.

c. The machine falls on the man.

d. The man looks around.

e. The man goes into room number 7.

f. The man wants to push the button on the machine.

g. The man walks down the hall.

D. Look at the pictures and the words. Circle the words you don't know. Ask the meaning. Match the pictures with the words. Write the correct letter in the box.

a. EMERGENCY
b. ENTRANCE
c. EXIT
d. NO SMOKING
e. DO NOT TOUCH
f. DO NOT ENTER
g. NO TRESPASSING
h. EMERGENCY EXIT

E. THREE IN A ROW. Look at the words again. Write one in each box. Play with a partner. Take turns. Read a word. Put a marker on the word. The winner has 3 markers in a row.

	DANGER	

NOTE: Students should write words on the Three in a Row board in random order.

F. Circle T for True or F for False.

1. The man opens the door to room number 4.   T   F

2. There is an ENTER sign beside the door.   T   F

3. The man walks down the hall.   T   F

4. The man enters room number 2.   T   F

5. The man sees a machine.   T   F

6. The man does not push the button.   T   F

7. A sign falls on the man.   T   F

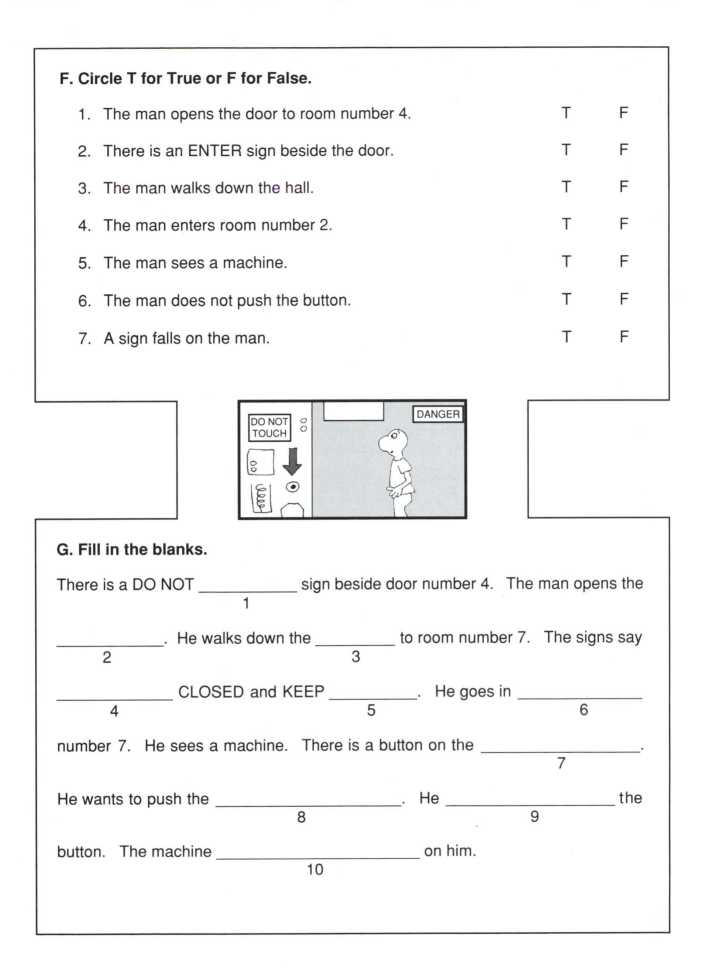

G. Fill in the blanks.

There is a DO NOT _____ sign beside door number 4.   The man opens the
                          1

_____.   He walks down the _____ to room number 7.   The signs say
     2   3

_____ CLOSED and KEEP _____.   He goes in _____
     4   5   6

number 7.   He sees a machine.   There is a button on the _____.
                                                                      7

He wants to push the _____.   He _____ the
                              8   9

button.   The machine _____ on him.
                              10

H. What do you think? Look at Exercise A. Answer these questions.

Where does the man go? Can the man read the signs? Why is the man looking behind him in Frame 8? What happens to the man? What signs are at your school or workplace? What do you do if you can't read these signs? What can the man do if he does not understand the signs?

I. Work with your teacher or a partner. Write words you remember from the story.

_____

Now write the story. Use the words to help you.

The Heater

A. Talk about the pictures.

NOTE: Discussion questions appear in Exercise H.

B. Number the pictures in order. Then tell the story.

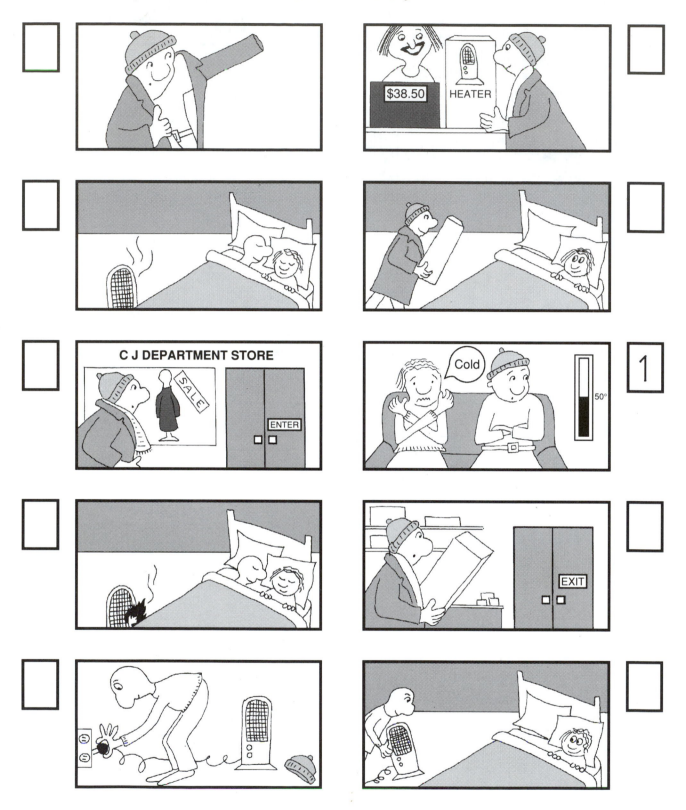

C. Match the picture with the sentence.

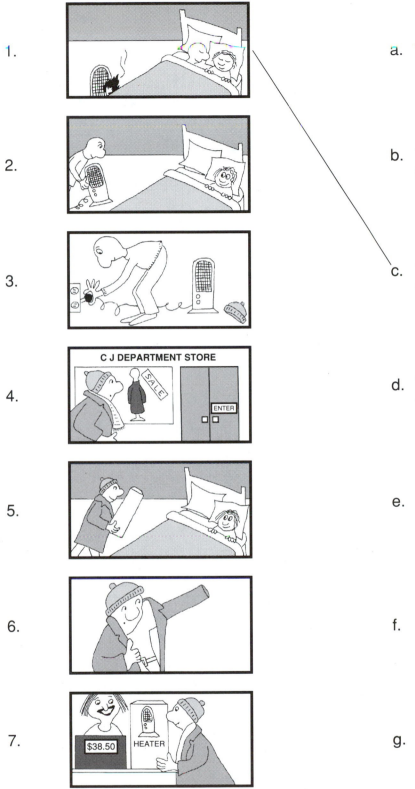

1.

2.

3.

4.

5.

6.

7.

a. The man puts on his coat.

b. The man takes the heater into the bedroom.

c. The man and the woman go to sleep. There's a fire.

d. The man puts the heater next to the bed.

e. The man goes to the department store.

f. The man buys a heater.

g. The man plugs in the heater.

D. Listen to the teacher. Circle the temperature you hear.

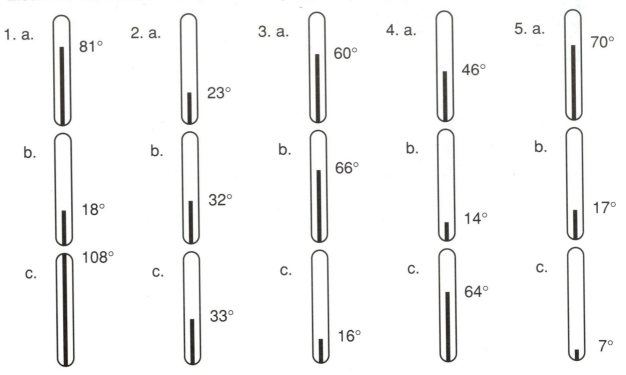

1. a. 81°
   b. 18°
   c. 108°

2. a. 23°
   b. 32°
   c. 33°

3. a. 60°
   b. 66°
   c. 16°

4. a. 46°
   b. 14°
   c. 64°

5. a. 70°
   b. 17°
   c. 7°

E. Listen to the temperature. Draw a line on the thermomometer.

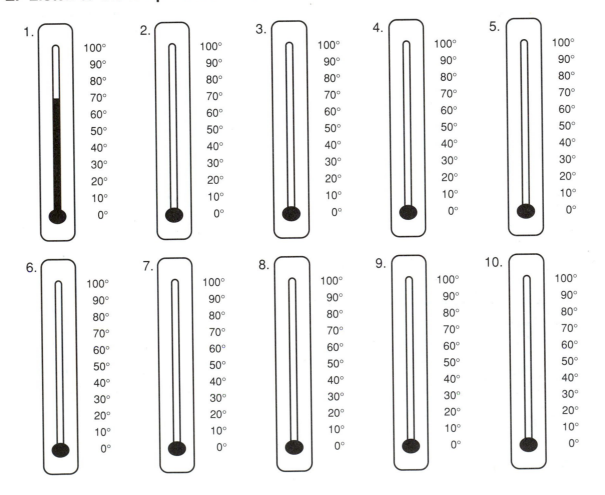

F. Circle T for True or F for False.

1. The man plugs in the heater.   T   F

2. There's a fire in the department store.   T   F

3. The man and the woman feel cold.   T   F

4. The man buys a heater for $38.50   T   F

5. The man and the woman go to sleep.   T   F

6. The woman goes to the department store.   T   F

7. The man puts his coat next to the bed.   T   F

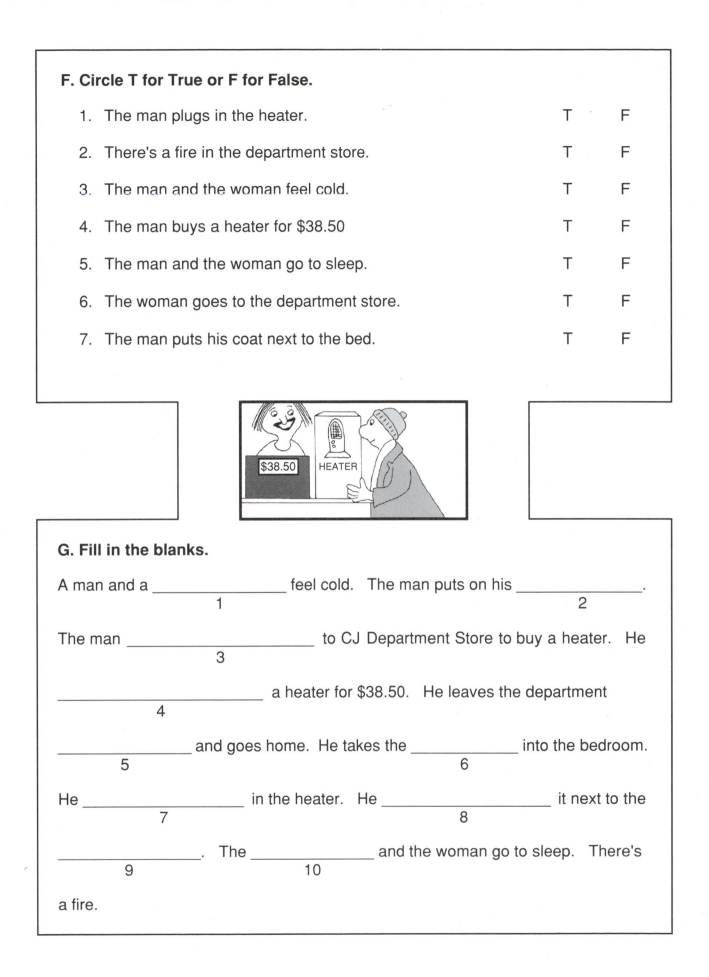

G. Fill in the blanks.

A man and a _____ feel cold. The man puts on his _____.
                    1   2

The man _____ to CJ Department Store to buy a heater. He
              3

_____ a heater for $38.50. He leaves the department
         4

_____ and goes home. He takes the _____ into the bedroom.
      5   6

He _____ in the heater. He _____ it next to the
         7   8

_____. The _____ and the woman go to sleep. There's
      9   10

a fire.

H. What do you think? Look at Exercise A. Answer these questions.

What does the man buy? Where does he put the heater? Why? What happens?
How do you heat your house? How much does it cost to heat your house? If the
man and woman's house is cold, what can they do? If the man and woman don't
have enough money to pay for heat, what can they do?

I. Work with your teacher or a partner. Write words you remember from the story.

_____

Now write the story. Use the words to help you.

House on Fire

A. Talk about the pictures.

NOTE: Discussion questions appear in Exercise H.

B. Number the pictures in order. Then tell the story.

C. Match the picture with the sentence.

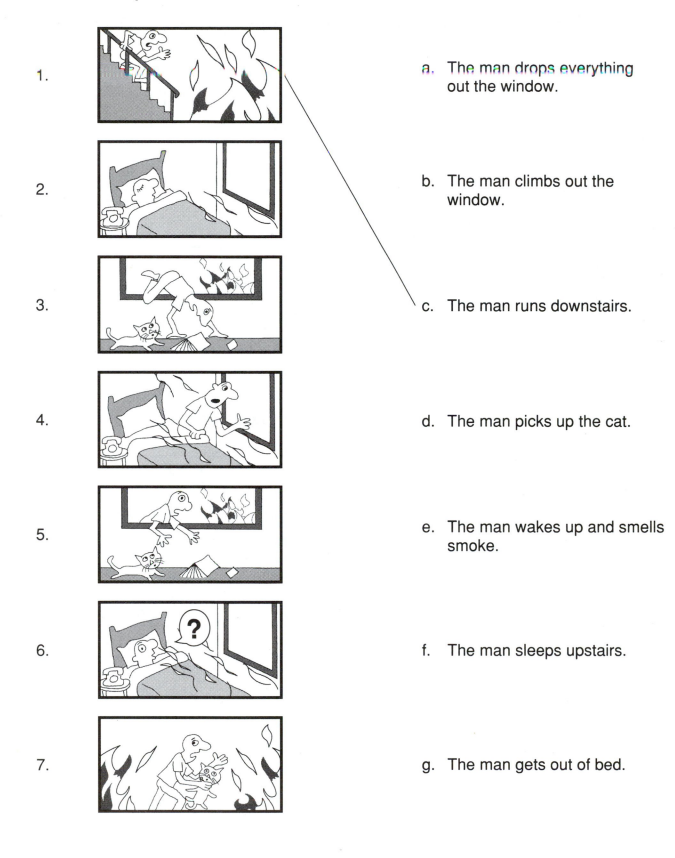

1.

2.

3.

4.

5.

6.

7.

a. The man drops everything out the window.

b. The man climbs out the window.

c. The man runs downstairs.

d. The man picks up the cat.

e. The man wakes up and smells smoke.

f. The man sleeps upstairs.

g. The man gets out of bed.

D. What do you save? Number your choices in order. 1 is the most important. Talk about your choices.

E. Listen to the teacher. Circle the place, address, and telephone number that you hear.

PLACE	ADDRESS	TELEPHONE
1. a. FIRE DEPARTMENT b. POLICE STATION c. AMBULANCE	a. 16 4th Street b. 4 7th Street c. 10 9th Street	a. 565–6231 b. 561–6535 c. 556–2630
2. a. AMBULANCE b. POLICE STATION c. FIRE DEPARTMENT	a. 30 L Street b. 14 D Street c. 3 B Street	a. 253–8960 b. 258–9800 c. 235–4890
3. a. POLICE STATION b. FIRE DEPARTMENT c. AMBULANCE	a. 10 6th Street b. 16 10th Street c. 4 1st Street	a. 381–6767 b. 318–2601 c. 813–7067
4. a. FIRE DEPARTMENT b. AMBULANCE c. POLICE STATION	a. 7 2nd Street b. 17 F Street c. 12 7th Street	a. 793–0400 b. 973–4000 c. 739–0040
5. a. POLICE STATION b. FIRE DEPARTMENT c. AMBULANCE	a. 20 2nd Street b. 2 3rd Street c. 9 5th Street	a. 848–8040 b. 488–4080 c. 484–4800

F. Circle T for True or F for False.

1. The man wakes up and smells smoke.   T   F

2. The man picks up the telephone.   T   F

3. The man drops his ID card out the window.   T   F

4. The man gets out of bed.   T   F

5. The man runs upstairs.   T   F

6. The man picks up his address book.   T   F

7. The man climbs out the window.   T   F

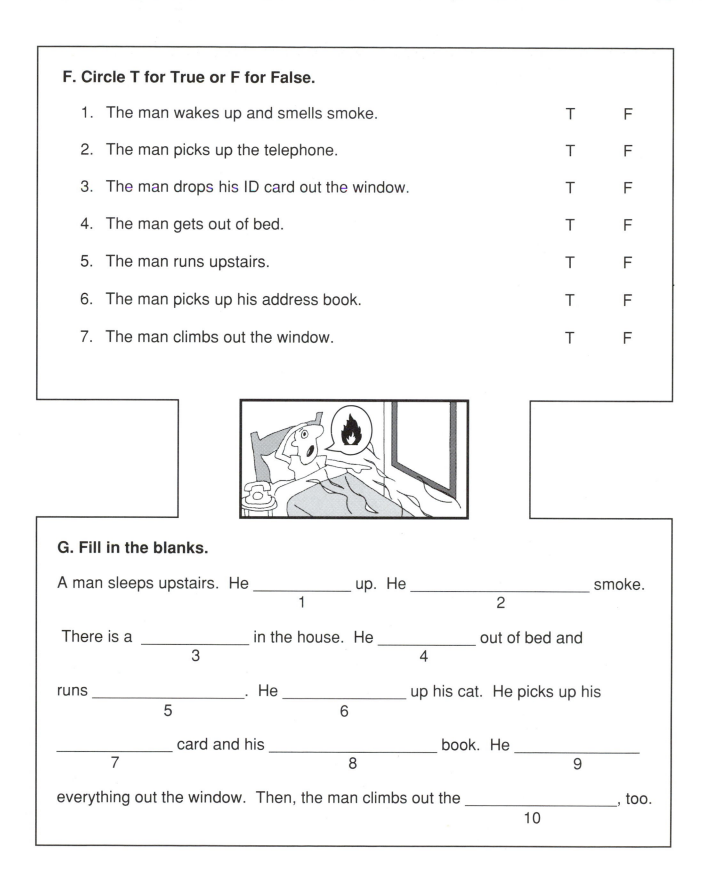

G. Fill in the blanks.

A man sleeps upstairs. He _____ up. He _____ smoke.
　　　　　　　　　　　　　　　　　1　　　　　　　　　　　　　　2

There is a _____ in the house. He _____ out of bed and
　　　　　　　　　3　　　　　　　　　　　　　　4

runs _____. He _____ up his cat. He picks up his
　　　　　　5　　　　　　　　　　　6

_____ card and his _____ book. He _____
　　　7　　　　　　　　　　　　8　　　　　　　　　　　　　　9

everything out the window. Then, the man climbs out the _____, too.
　　　　　　　　　　　　　　　　　　　　　　　　　　　　　　10

H. What do you think? Look at Exercise A. Answer these questions.

What does the man do when he smells smoke? What does he save from the fire?
How do you think the fire started? How can fires start? What can you do if a fire
starts in your house? What would you save?

I. Work with your teacher or a partner. Write words you remember from the story.

_____

Now write the story. Use the words to help you.

The Job Interview

A. Talk about the pictures.

NOTE: Discussion questions appear in Exercise H.

B. Number the pictures in order. Then tell the story.

C. Match the picture with the sentence.

1.

2.

3.

4.

5.

6.

7.

a. The man and the woman look in the newspaper for jobs.

b. The man and the woman both say, "I want a job."

c. The man and the woman go to the offices at the grocery stores.

d. The man and the woman give the employers their job applications.

e. The man and the woman look at the ads for two jobs.

f. The man and the woman fill out job applications.

g. On Monday the woman starts her job. Her husband is looking for a job again.

D. Look at these words. Circle the words you don't know. Ask the meaning.

last	zip code	place
first	area code	from/to
middle	social security number	employment
	education	signature

E. JOB APPLICATION. You want a job. Fill in the blanks on this form.

Date _____

Name _____ , _____ _____
          (last)   (first)   (middle)

Address _____
             (street)

     _____ , _____ _____
       (city)   (state)   (zip code)

Telephone _____ — _____ — _____
        (area code)

Social Securtiy Number _____ — _____ — _____

Education

1. _____ _____ _____
    (school)   (place)   (from/to)

2. _____ _____ _____
    (school)   (place)   (from/to)

Employment

1. _____ _____ _____
    (job)   (place)   (from/to)

2. _____ _____ _____
    (job)   (place)   (from/to)

                             _____
                               (Signature)

F. Circle T for True or F for False.

1. The man does not look for a job.   T   F

2. The employer asks questions in the interview.   T   F

3. The man and the woman fill out job applications.   T   F

4. The employer tells the woman to start work on Monday.   T   F

5. The woman gets a job at M and N Grocery.   T   F

6. The man gets a job at G and D Grocery.   T   F

7. The woman doesn't get a job.   T   F

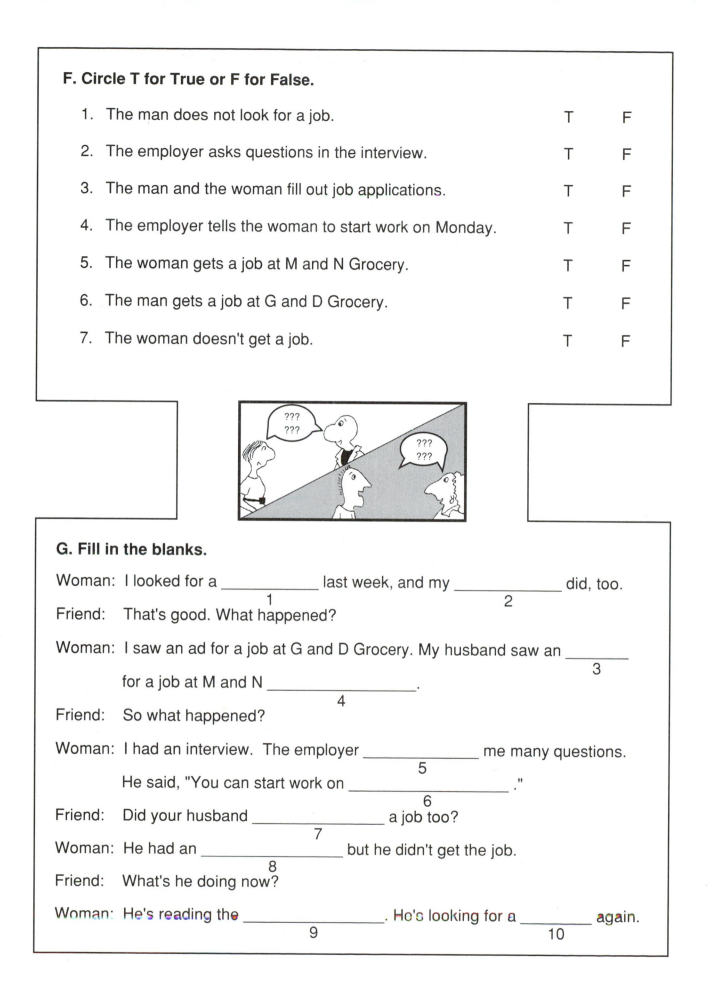

G. Fill in the blanks.

Woman: I looked for a _____ last week, and my _____ did, too.
                               1   2

Friend: That's good. What happened?

Woman: I saw an ad for a job at G and D Grocery. My husband saw an _____
                                                                               3

        for a job at M and N _____.
                                            4

Friend: So what happened?

Woman: I had an interview. The employer _____ me many questions.
                                                      5

        He said, "You can start work on _____."
                                              6

Friend: Did your husband _____ a job too?
                                     7

Woman: He had an _____ but he didn't get the job.
                             8

Friend: What's he doing now?

Woman: He's reading the _____. He's looking for a _____ again.
                               9   10

H. What do you think? Look at Exercise A. Answer these questions.

What does the man want? What does the woman want? Who gets the job? How does the man feel? Were you ever turned down for a job? How did you feel? What can the man do now?

I. Work with your teacher or a partner. Write words you remember from the story.

Now write the story. Use the words to help you.

No Exit

A. Talk about the pictures.

NOTE: Discussion questions appear in Exercise H.

B. Number the pictures in order. Then tell the story.

C. Match the picture with the sentence.

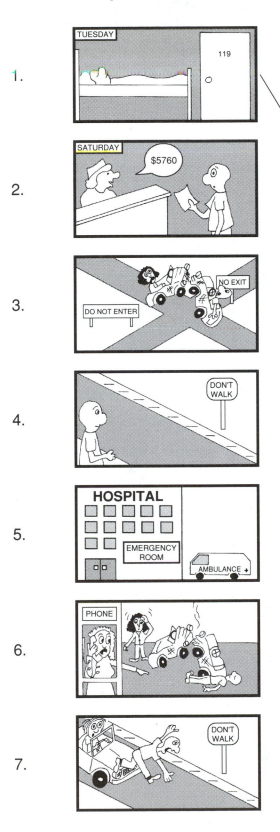

1.

2.

3.

4.

5.

6.

7.

a. Two cars have an accident.

b. A woman sees the accident. She calls an ambulance.

c. The man is in bed.

d. An ambulance takes the man to the hospital.

e. The man owes a lot of money.

f. The man is on the sidewalk. The sign says DON'T WALK.

g. The man crosses the street. A car hits him.

D. Look at the pictures and the words. Circle the words you don't know. Ask the meaning. Match the pictures with the words. Write the correct letter in the box.

a. DON'T WALK
b. NO SMOKING
c. ENTRANCE
d. EXIT
e. AMBULANCE
f. EMERGENCY ROOM
g. DO NOT ENTER
h. HOSPITAL

1. b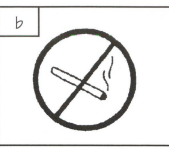

2.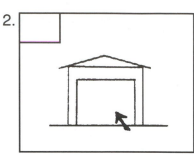

3.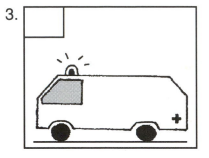

4.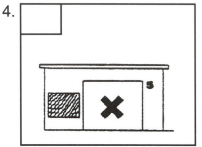

5.

6.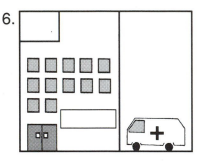

7.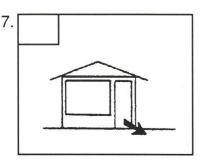

8.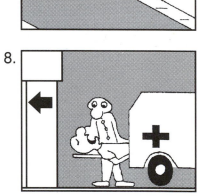

E. THREE IN A ROW. Look at the words again. Write one in each box. Play with a partner. Take turns. Read a word. Put a marker on the word. The winner has 3 markers in a row.

	NO EXIT	

NOTE: Students should write words on the Three in a Row board in random order.

F. Circle T for True or F for False.

1. The man has two accidents.   T   F

2. A woman gets in an ambulance.   T   F

3. The man goes to the emergency room.   T   F

4. The man is in room 5760.   T   F

5. The man leaves the hospital on Saturday.   T   F

6. The man owes a lot of money.   T   F

7. The street sign says WALK.   T   F

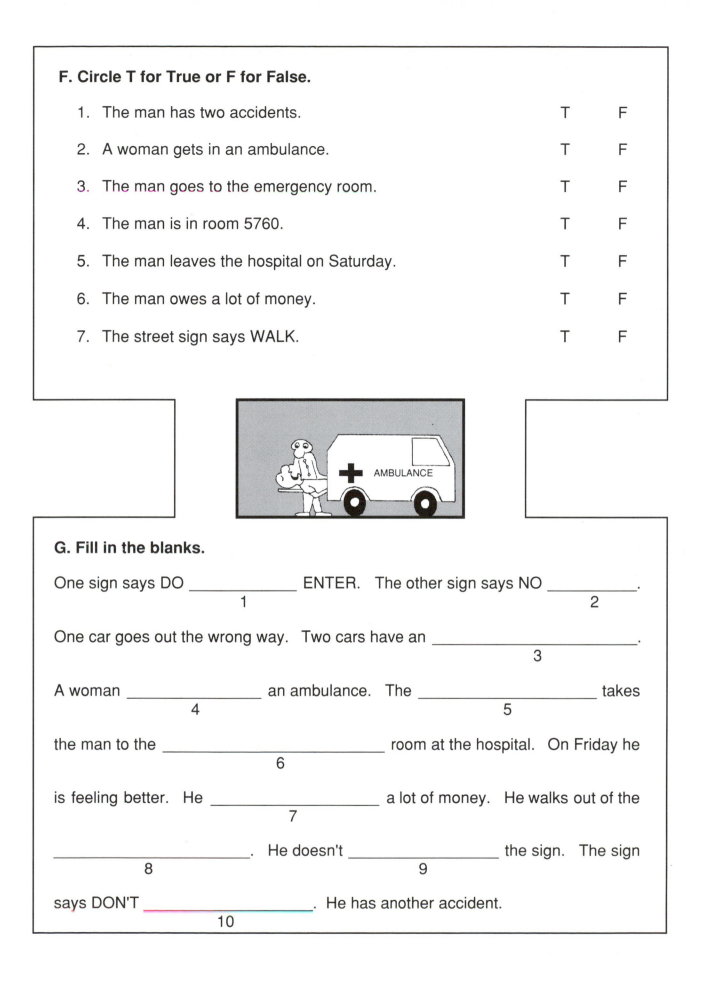

G. Fill in the blanks.

One sign says DO _____ ENTER.   The other sign says NO _____.
                          1   2

One car goes out the wrong way. Two cars have an _____.
                                                                            3

A woman _____ an ambulance. The _____ takes
                    4   5

the man to the _____ room at the hospital. On Friday he
                                    6

is feeling better. He _____ a lot of money. He walks out of the
                                    7

_____. He doesn't _____ the sign. The sign
              8   9

says DON'T _____. He has another accident.
                        10

H. What do you think? Look at Exercise A. Answer these questions.

What happens to the man? Why did he have the first accident? Why did he have the second accident? Do you think he can read? What signs do you read on the way to school or work? Do you know anyone who can't read signs? What happens when a person can't read signs? What can a person do if he can't read?

I. Work with your teacher or a partner. Write words you remember from the story.

_____

Now write the story. Use the words to help you.

OK, No Job

A. Talk about the pictures.

NOTE: Discussion questions appear in Exercise G.

B. Number the pictures in order. Then tell the story.

C. Match the picture with the sentence.

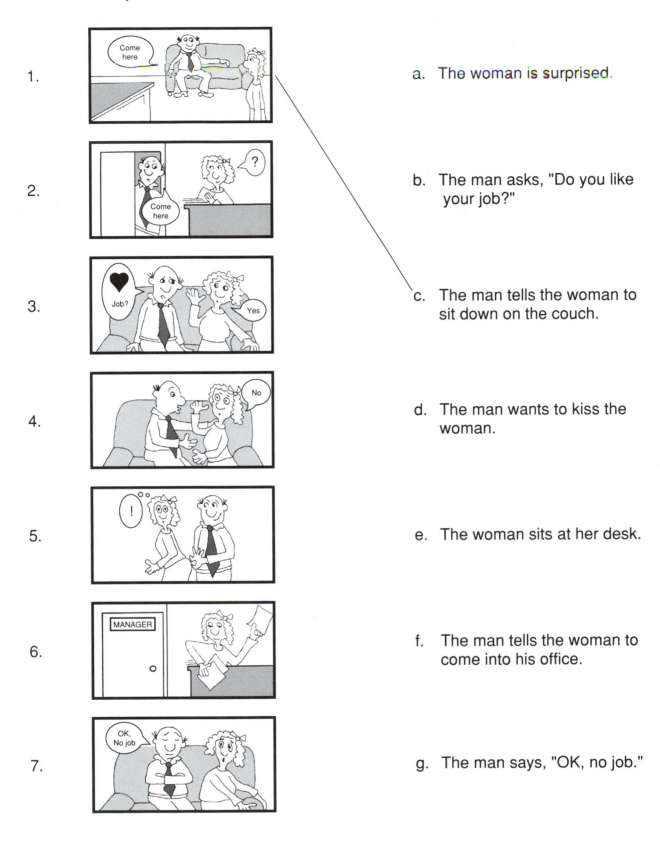

1.

a. The woman is surprised.

2.

b. The man asks, "Do you like your job?"

3.

c. The man tells the woman to sit down on the couch.

4.

d. The man wants to kiss the woman.

5.

e. The woman sits at her desk.

6.

f. The man tells the woman to come into his office.

7.

g. The man says, "OK, no job."

D. What is OK to do at work? Check the activities that are OK at work.

	OK IN MY COUNTRY	OK IN U.S.
1.	_____	_____
2.	_____	_____
3.	_____	_____
4.	_____	_____
5.	_____	_____
6.	_____	_____
7.	_____	_____
8.	_____	_____
9.	_____	_____

E. Circle T for True or F for False.

1. The woman is a secretary.   T   F

2. The man kisses the woman.   T   F

3. The woman likes her job.   T   F

4. The man pinches the woman.   T   F

5. The woman wants to kiss the man.   T   F

6. The woman sits down next to the man.   T   F

7. The man is the woman's boss.   T   F

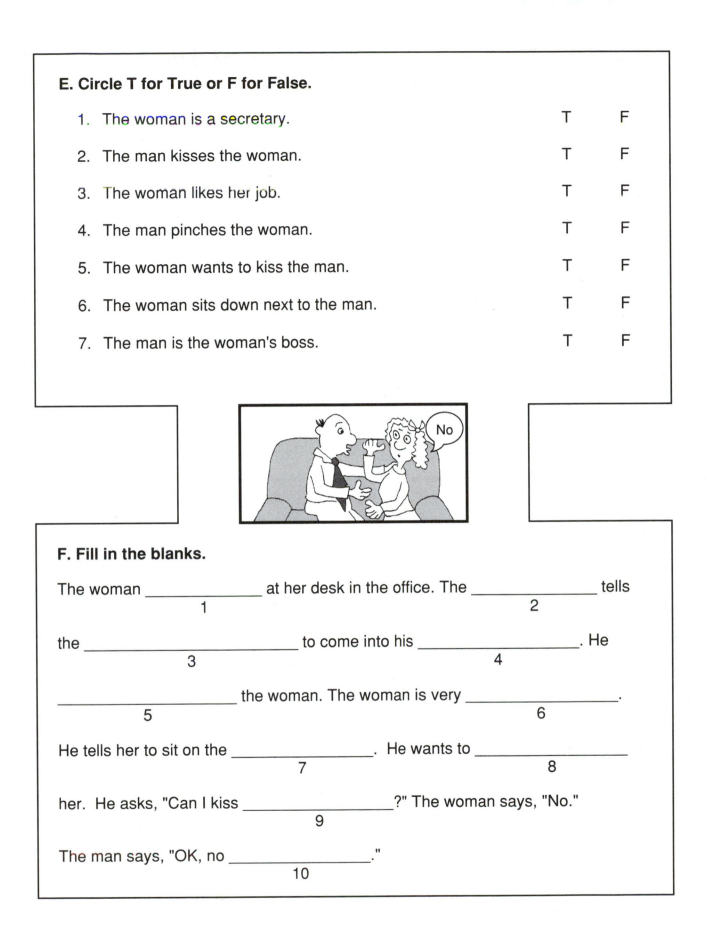

F. Fill in the blanks.

The woman _____ at her desk in the office. The _____ tells
                1   2

the _____ to come into his _____. He
              3   4

_____ the woman. The woman is very _____.
              5   6

He tells her to sit on the _____. He wants to _____
                       7   8

her. He asks, "Can I kiss _____?" The woman says, "No."
                          9

The man says, "OK, no _____."
                     10

G. What do you think? Look at Exercise A. Answer these questions.

What does the manager want? Look at Frame 3. What is the woman asking her boss? What happens to the woman? How does the woman feel? Did this ever happen to you or anyone you know? What can the woman do in this situation?

H. Work with your teacher or a partner. Write words you remember from the story.

Now write the story. Use the words to help you.

A. Talk about the pictures.

NOTE: Discussion questions appear in Exercise H.

B. Number the pictures in order. Then tell the story.

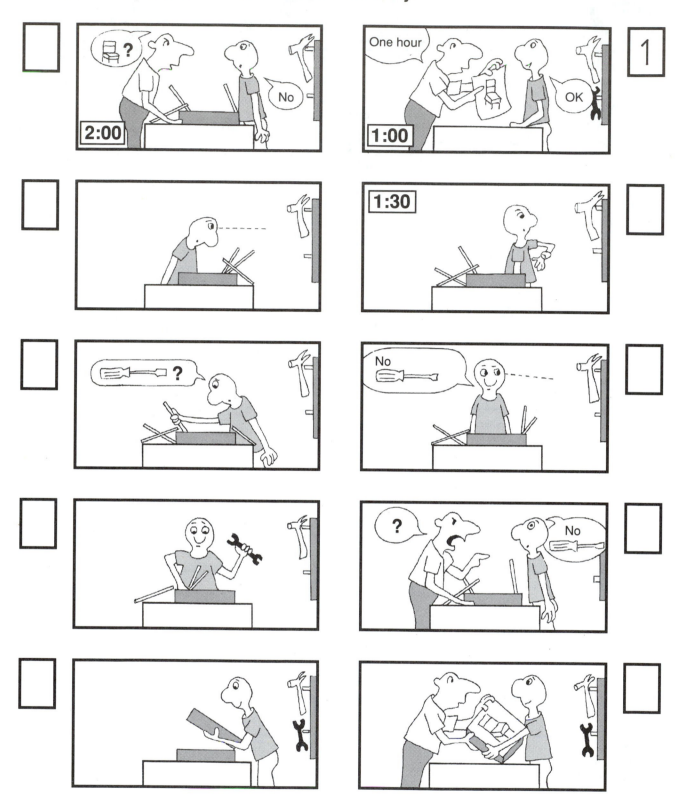

C. Match the picture with the sentence.

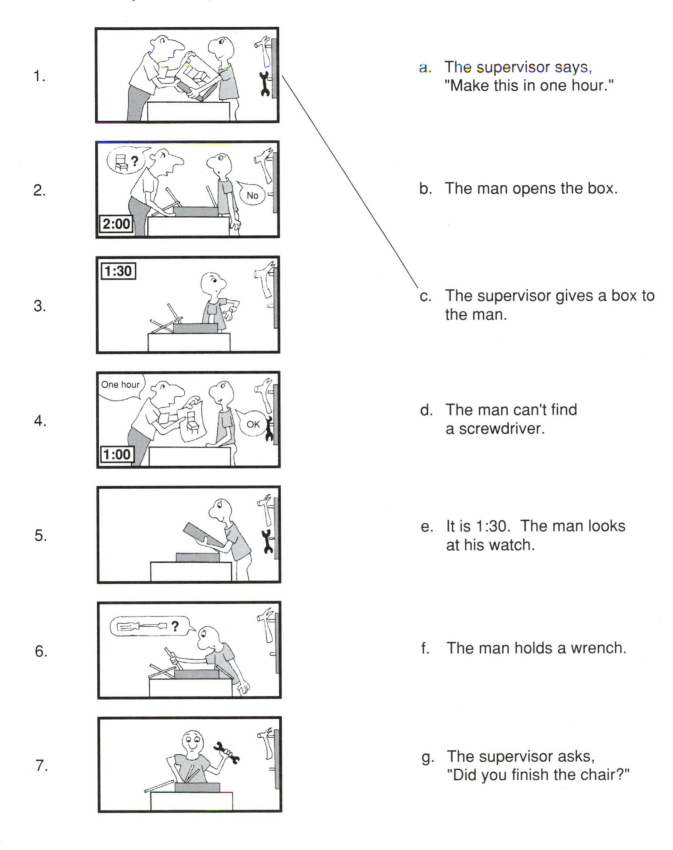

1.

2.

3.

4.

5.

6.

7.

a. The supervisor says,
    "Make this in one hour."

b. The man opens the box.

c. The supervisor gives a box to
    the man.

d. The man can't find
    a screwdriver.

e. It is 1:30. The man looks
    at his watch.

f. The man holds a wrench.

g. The supervisor asks,
    "Did you finish the chair?"

D. Listen to the teacher. Circle the time you hear. Then write the time in the blank.

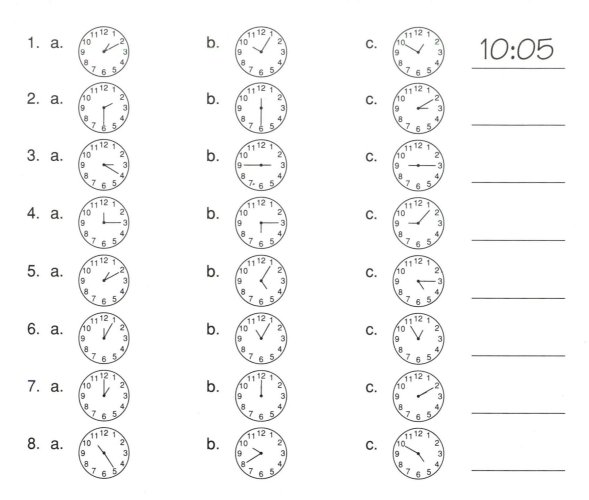

1. a.   b.   c.   10:05

2. a.   b.   c.   _____

3. a.   b.   c.   _____

4. a.   b.   c.   _____

5. a.   b.   c.   _____

6. a.   b.   c.   _____

7. a.   b.   c.   _____

8. a.   b.   c.   _____

E. THREE IN A ROW. Look at the times above. Write one time in each box. Play with a partner. Take turns. Read a time. Put a marker on the time. The winner has three markers in a row.

	1:10	

NOTE: Students should write times on the Three in a Row board in random order.

F. Circle T for True or F for False.

1. The man takes pieces of a chair out of a box.   T   F

2. The man makes a chair.   T   F

3. There is a screwdriver in the box.   T   F

4. The man waits for dinner.   T   F

5. The supervisor gives the man a picture of a chair.   T   F

6. The supervisor needs the chair in one hour.   T   F

7. The supervisor is angry.   T   F

G. Fill in the blanks.

It is 1:00. A supervisor gives a man a picture. The supervisor says, "Make this

_____ in one hour." The man opens a _____. The man takes
         1   2

out the _____ of the chair. He needs a screwdriver. He can't find a
                    3

_____. It's 1:30. He waits. At _____
                    4   5

the supervisor comes again. The _____ asks, "Did
                                                                            6

you finish the _____?" The man _____, "No."
                          7   8

The supervisor is _____. He asks, "Why?" The man says, "I can't
                                9

_____ a screwdriver."
            10

H. What do you think? Look at Exercise A. Answer these questions.

Does the man make the chair? Why does he wait? Does the man ask any questions? What do you do if you don't understand something in school or at your workplace?

I. Work with your teacher or a partner. Write words you remember from the story.

_____

Now write the story. Use the words to help you.

A. Talk about the pictures.

NOTE: Discussion questions appear in Exercise H.

B. Number the pictures in order. Then tell the story.

C. Match the picture with the sentence.

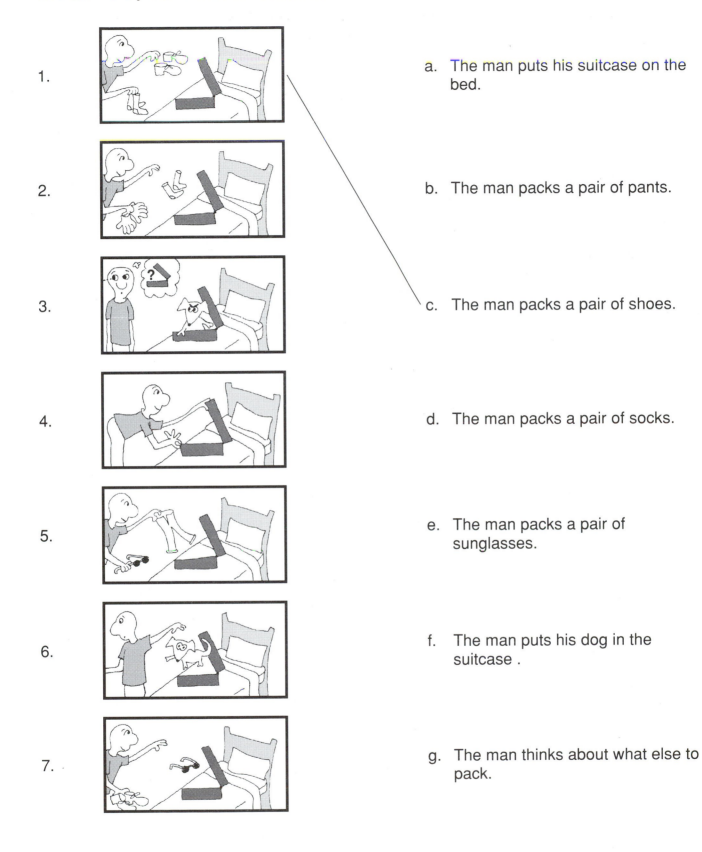

1.

2.

3.

4.

5.

6.

7.

a. The man puts his suitcase on the bed.

b. The man packs a pair of pants.

c. The man packs a pair of shoes.

d. The man packs a pair of socks.

e. The man packs a pair of sunglasses.

f. The man puts his dog in the suitcase .

g. The man thinks about what else to pack.

D. Look at these words. Circle the words you don't know. Ask the meaning.

pair of shoes   pair of pants   pair of sunglasses   dog
pair of socks   pair of underwear   pair of gloves

E. THE PACKING GAME. Play with a partner. One is A. One is B. Take turns. Throw one of the dice. Move your marker. Look at the picture. What are you going to pack?
Player A: Find the word in Box A. Put an X by the word. **Player B:** Find the word in Box B. Put an X by the word. The winner has the most X's.

Start

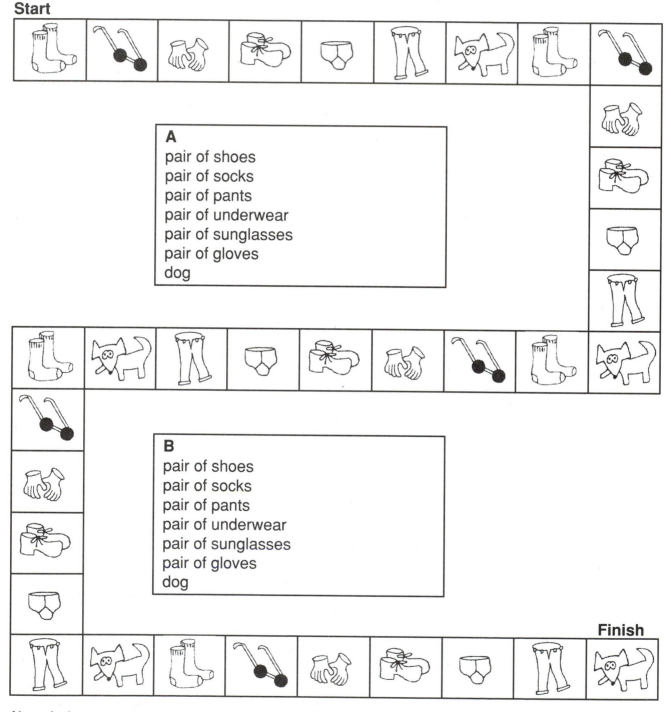

A
pair of shoes
pair of socks
pair of pants
pair of underwear
pair of sunglasses
pair of gloves
dog

B
pair of shoes
pair of socks
pair of pants
pair of underwear
pair of sunglasses
pair of gloves
dog

Finish

Note: A player can put more than one X next to each word. Players only go around once. A player who reaches the finish box waits for the other player to complete the game.

F. Circle T for True or F for False.

1. The man packs his suitcase in the bedroom.   T   F

2. The suitcase is under the bed.   T   F

3. The man packs one pair of pants.   T   F

4. The man packs two pairs of socks.   T   F

5. The man packs the dog in his suitcase.   T   F

6. The man is going to college.   T   F

7. The man packs one glove.   T   F

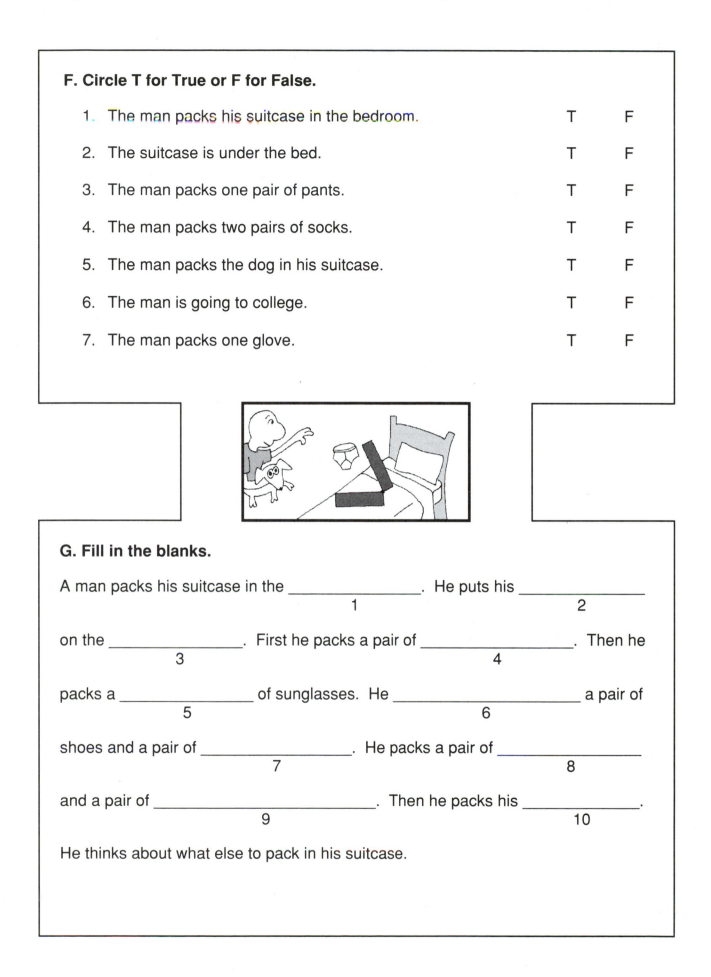

G. Fill in the blanks.

A man packs his suitcase in the _____. He puts his _____
                                   1   2

on the _____. First he packs a pair of _____. Then he
               3   4

packs a _____ of sunglasses. He _____ a pair of
             5   6

shoes and a pair of _____. He packs a pair of _____
                    7   8

and a pair of _____. Then he packs his _____.
               9   10

He thinks about what else to pack in his suitcase.

H. What do you think? Look at Exercise A. Answer these questions.

Where is the man going? What does he pack? Do you know someone who is in college? How does someone get into college? How much does it cost to go to college? Do you or someone you know want to go to college? What do you need to do?

I. Work with your teacher or a partner. Write words you remember from the story.

_____

_____

Now write the story. Use the words to help you.

UNIT 13

Pancakes

A. Talk about the pictures. Then listen to the story.

NOTE: Discussion questions appear in Exercise H.

Pancakes   73

C. Match the picture with the sentence.

1.

2.

3.

4.

5.

6.

7.

a. The woman puts 2 cups of flour in the bowl.

b. The woman reads 1 TSP SUGAR.

c. The woman bakes the pancakes in the oven.

d. The dog eats the pancakes.

e. The woman reads MIX and FRY.

f. The woman puts 1 cup of sugar in the bowl.

g. The friend says, "Good!"

D. Look at these words. Circle the words you don't know. Ask the meaning.

CUP	TSP	TBSP	EGGS	OIL
FLOUR	SUGAR	SALT	MILK	

E. THE INGREDIENTS GAME. Play with a partner. One is A. One is B. Take turns. Throw one of the dice. Move your marker. What are you going to use to cook? **Player A:** Write the amount and the ingredient in Box A. **Player B:** Write the amount and the ingredient in Box B. The winner has the recipe closest to the pancake recipe in Exercise A.

Start

1 CUP FLOUR	2 CUPS FLOUR	3 CUPS FLOUR	1 TSP SUGAR	1 TBSP SUGAR	1 CUP SUGAR	1 TSP SALT	1 TBSP SALT	1 CUP SALT

A   Amount   Ingredient

1. _____ _____
2. _____ _____
3. _____ _____
4. _____ _____
5. _____ _____
6. _____ _____
7. _____ _____

2 EGGS

3 EGGS

4 EGGS

1 CUP MILK

1 TSP SUGAR	1 CUP FLOUR	3 CUPS FLOUR	2 CUPS FLOUR	1 CUP FLOUR	1 TBSP OIL	1 TSP OIL	3 CUPS MILK	2 CUPS MILK

1 TBSP SUGAR

1 CUP SUGAR

1 TSP SALT

1 TBSP SALT

B   Amount   Ingredient

1. _____ _____
2. _____ _____
3. _____ _____
4. _____ _____
5. _____ _____
6. _____ _____
7. _____ _____

Finish

1 CUP SALT	2 EGGS	3 EGGS	4 EGGS	1 CUP MILK	2 CUPS MILK	3 CUPS MILK	1 TSP OIL	1 TBSP OIL

Note: A player can write an ingredient more than once. Players only go around once. A player who reaches the finish box waits for the other player to complete the game.

F. Circle T for True or F for False.

1. The woman reads a recipe for pancakes.   T   F

2. The woman puts 1 tsp. of sugar in the bowl.   T   F

3. The woman reads 3 CUPS OF MILK.   T   F

4. The woman fries the pancakes.   T   F

5. The woman bakes the pancakes in the oven.   T   F

6. Her friend likes the pancakes.   T   F

7. Her friend gives the pancakes to the dog.   T   F

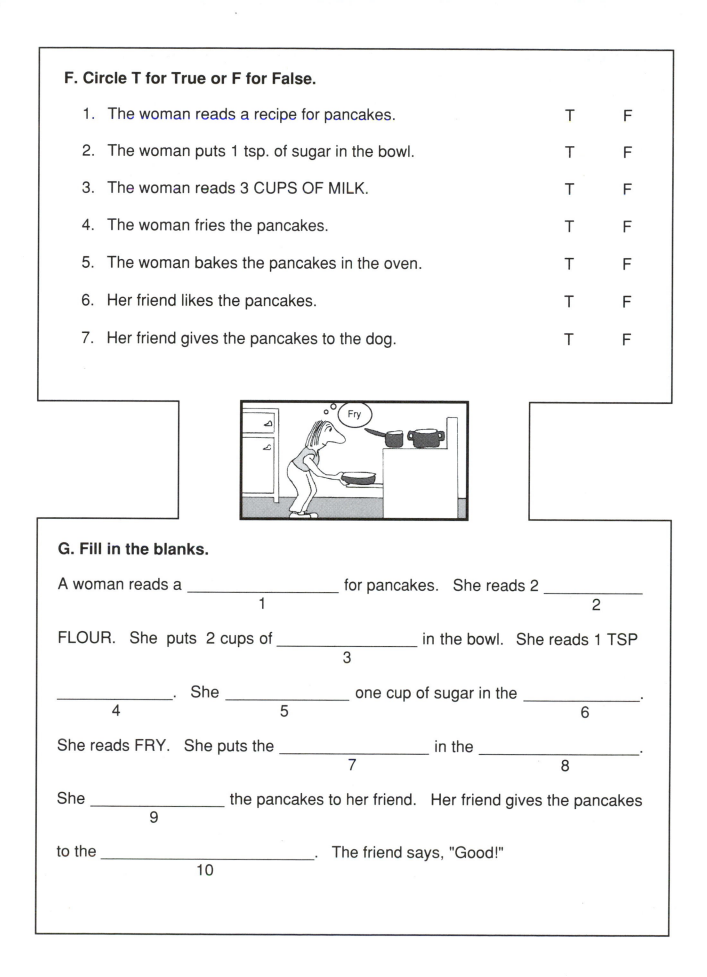

G. Fill in the blanks.

A woman reads a _____ for pancakes. She reads 2 _____
                    1   2

FLOUR. She puts 2 cups of _____ in the bowl. She reads 1 TSP
                                    3

_____. She _____ one cup of sugar in the _____.
       4   5   6

She reads FRY. She puts the _____ in the _____.
                                  7   8

She _____ the pancakes to her friend. Her friend gives the pancakes
         9

to the _____. The friend says, "Good!"
         10

H. What do you think? Look at Exercise A. Answer these questions.

What mistakes does the woman make? Why does she make the mistakes?
Does her friend like the pancakes? Is there any American food that you do
not like? What? Where did you eat it? What did you do? What did you say?
What else could the friend in this story do?

I. Work with your teacher or a partner. Write words you remember from the story.

_____

Now write the story. Use the words to help you.

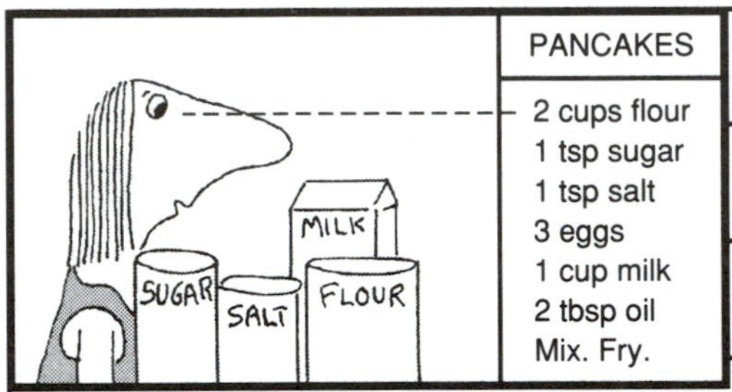

PANCAKES	
2 cups flour	
1 tsp sugar	
1 tsp salt	
3 eggs	
1 cup milk	
2 tbsp oil	
Mix. Fry.	

Good

Stay for Dinner

A. Talk about the pictures.

NOTE: Discussion questions appear in Exercise H.

B. Number the pictures in order. Then tell the story.

C. Match the picture with the sentence.

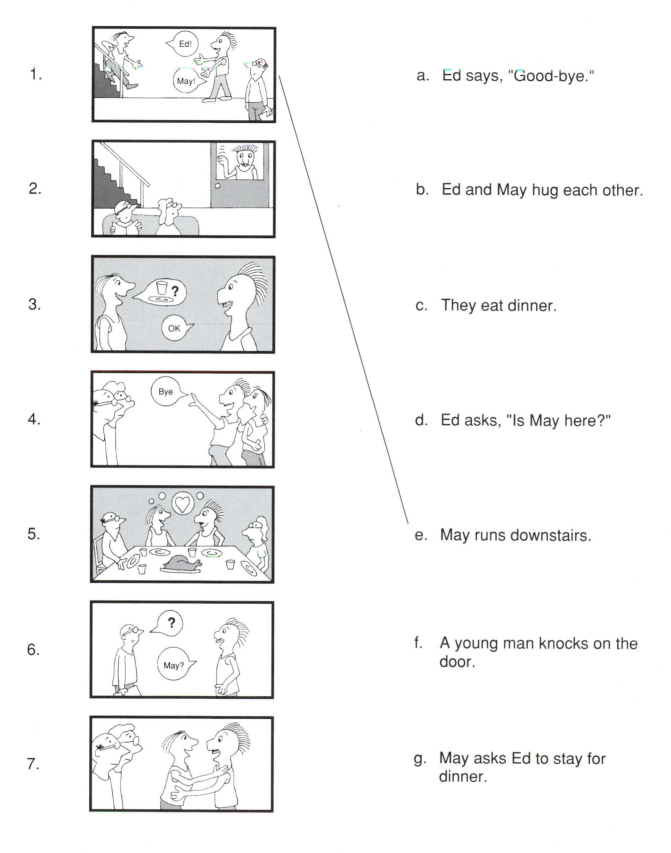

1.

2.

3.

4.

5.

6.

7.

a. Ed says, "Good-bye."

b. Ed and May hug each other.

c. They eat dinner.

d. Ed asks, "Is May here?"

e. May runs downstairs.

f. A young man knocks on the door.

g. May asks Ed to stay for dinner.

D. CROSSWORD PUZZLE. Look at the pictures of the family. Write these words in the boxes: daughter, father, husband, mother, son, wife.

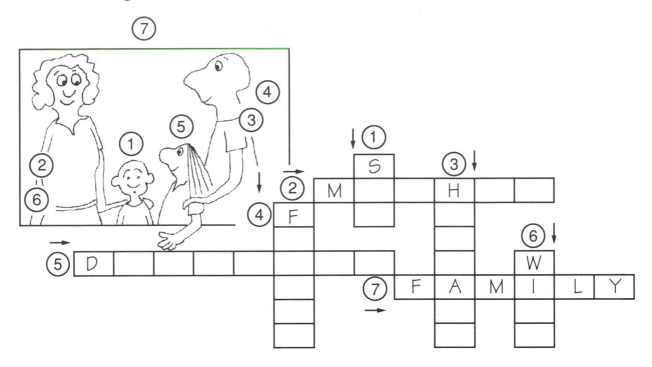

E. Please come to dinner. Listen to the teacher. Circle the day, time and address you hear.

DAY	TIME	ADDRESS

1. a. Monday
   b. Wednesday
   c. Thursday
	a. 7:30 p.m.
	b. 6:00 p.m.
	c. 8:30 a.m.
		a. 1 3rd Street
		b. 30 1st Street
		c. 3 3rd Street

2. a. Tuesday
   b. Thursday
   c. Saturday
	a. 7:30 p.m.
	b. 9:00 p.m.
	c. 8:00 p.m.
		a. 7 2nd Street
		b. 17 1st Street
		c. 70 3rd Street

3. a. Wednesday
   b. Tuesday
   c. Sunday
	a. 10:30 a.m.
	b. 6:30 p.m.
	c. 7:30 p.m.
		a. 4 5th Street
		b. 14 5th Street
		c. 40 5th Street

4. a. Friday
   b. Monday
   c. Saturday
	a. 6:30 p.m.
	b. 3:00 p.m.
	c. 7:00 p.m.
		a. 16 4th Street
		b. 60 1st Street
		c. 50 3rd Street

5. a. Sunday
   b. Saturday
   c. Thursday
	a. 6:00 p.m.
	b. 8:00 p.m.
	c. 7:00 p.m.
		a. 2 1st Street
		b. 12 7th Street
		c. 7 2nd Street

F. Circle T for True or F for False.

1. May's mother and father are angry.   T   F

2. Ed and May eat outside.   T   F

3. May's mother calls upstairs.   T   F

4. Ed and May kiss each other.   T   F

5. May's mother asks, "Do you want to stay for dinner?"   T   F

6. May's father is downstairs.   T   F

7. May goes upstairs.   T   F

G. Fill in the blanks.

A young man knocks on the door. He asks, "Is May here?" May's _____
                                                                  1

calls May. May is upstairs. May hears her father. She runs _____.
                                                                  2

May and Ed are happy. They hug each _____ . May's _____
                                        3   4

and father are surprised. May asks Ed, "Do you _____ to stay for
                                                        5

dinner?" Ed says, "OK." After they eat _____ Ed says, "_____."
                                            6   7

Ed and May _____ outside. They _____ each other. May's mother
                  8   9

and father are _____.
                      10

H. What do you think? Look at Exercise A. Answer these questions.

How does May feel about Ed? How do May's parents feel about Ed? Why? Are you or someone you know in love with someone your family doesn't like? What can you do? What can your friends do? What should May's parents do? Should May obey her parent's wishes?

I. Work with your teacher or a partner. Write words you remember from the story.

_____

Now write the story. Use the words to help you.

The Toaster

A. Talk about the pictures.

NOTE: Discussion questions appear in Exercise H.

B. Number the pictures in order. Then tell the story.

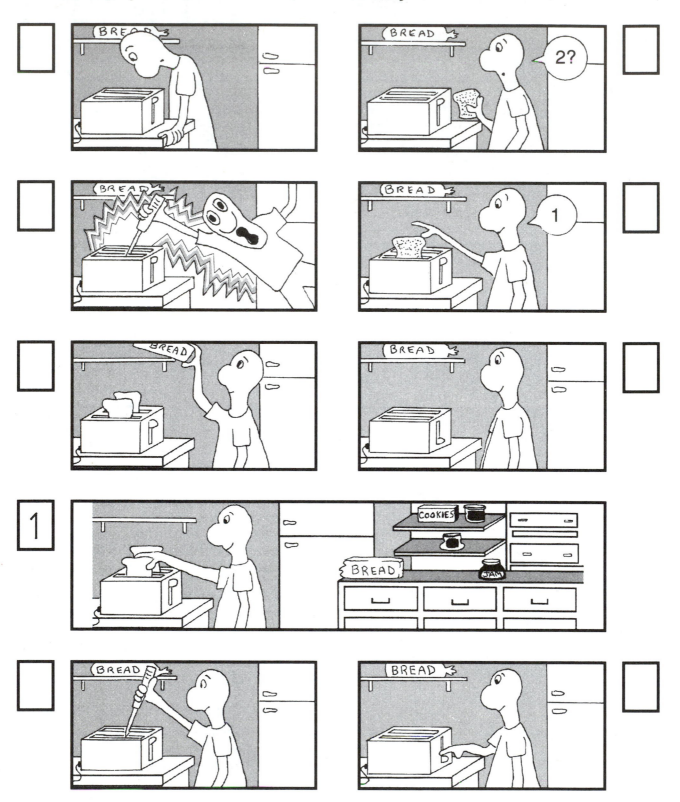

C. Match the picture with the sentence.

1.

2.

3.

4.

5.

6.

7.

a. The man puts a knife in the toaster.

b. The man looks in the toaster.

c. The man waits for the toast.

d. The man asks, "Where is the second piece?"

e. The man puts a piece of bread in the toaster.

f. The man puts away the loaf of bread on the shelf.

g. The man gets a shock.

D. Listen to the teacher. Draw a line from the picture to the correct shelf.

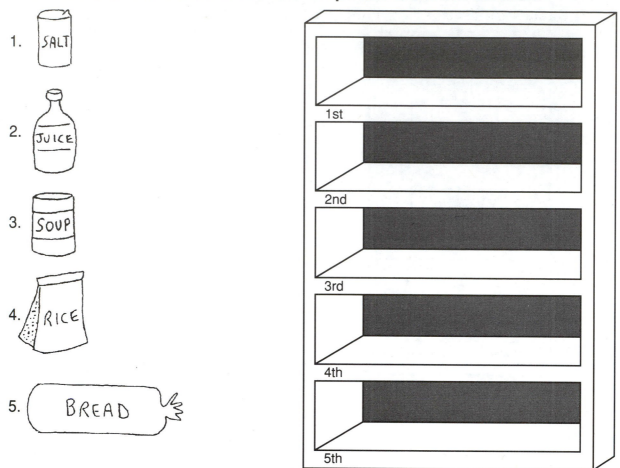

1. SALT

2. JUICE

3. SOUP

4. RICE

5. BREAD

1st

2nd

3rd

4th

5th

E. Match the picture with the number. Match the number with the word.

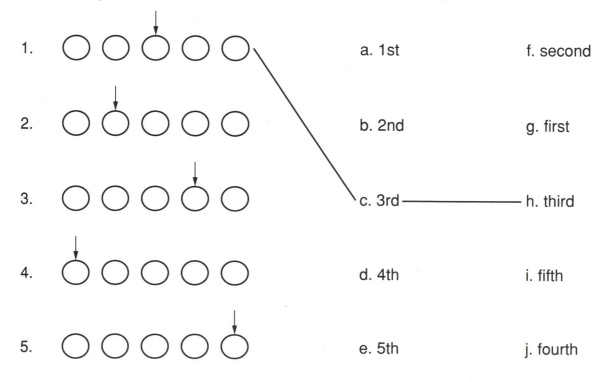

1.

2.

3.

4.

5.

a. 1st   f. second

b. 2nd   g. first

c. 3rd ———— h. third

d. 4th   i. fifth

e. 5th   j. fourth

F. Circle T for True or F for False.

1. The man gets a shock from the toaster.   T   F

2. He picks up the toaster.   T   F

3. He pushes a loaf of bread into the toaster.   T   F

4. He waits for the second piece of toast.   T   F

5. Only one piece of toast comes up.   T   F

6. He puts away the knife.   T   F

7. The man asks, "Where is the first piece of toast?"   T   F

G. Fill in the blanks.

A man puts a piece of bread into the _____ . He puts in a
                                            1

second _____ of bread. He puts away the loaf of _____.
              2   3

He puts the bread on the _____ . He _____ for the
                                4   5

toast to come up.   The first piece of toast _____ up. He asks, "Where is
                                                        6

the _____ piece of _____?" He _____
            7   8   9

up a knife. He puts the _____ in the toaster. He gets a shock.
                                10

H. What do you think? Look at Exercise A. Answer these questions.

Why does the man put the knife in the toaster? What happens? What other appliances can be dangerous? Did you or someone you know ever have an accident with an appliance? How can the man get the toast out of the toaster safely?

I. Work with your teacher or a partner. Write words you remember from the story.

_____

Now write the story. Use the words to help you.

UNIT 16 The Wallet

A. Talk about the pictures.

NOTE: Discussion questions appear in Exercise G.

The Wallet   91

B. Number the pictures in order. Then tell the story.

C. Match the picture with the sentence.

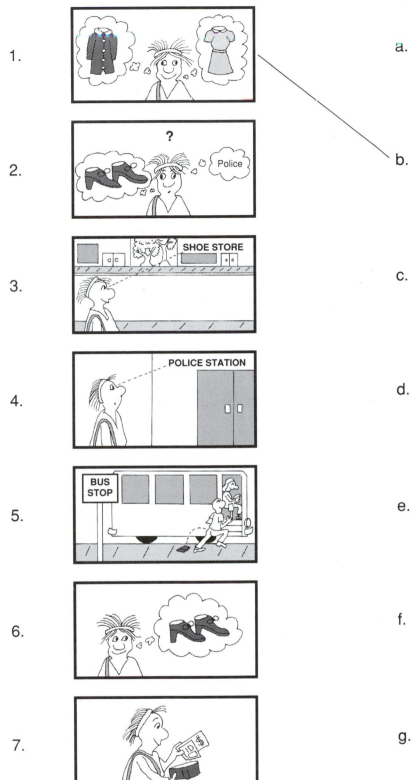

1.

2.

3.

4.

5.

6.

7.

a. The wallet falls out of the man's pocket.

b. The woman wants to buy a new coat or a new dress.

c. The woman sees the ID and the money in the wallet.

d. The woman sees the police station.

e. The woman thinks about what to do.

f. The woman sees the shoe store.

g. The woman wants to buy a new pair of shoes.

The Wallet   93

D. THE MAP GAME. Play with a partner. You are A. Your partner is B.
Listen to your partner's question. Look at your map. Answer the
question. Then look at your box. Where is bus number 6? Ask your
partner. Listen to the answer. Write the street name in your box.

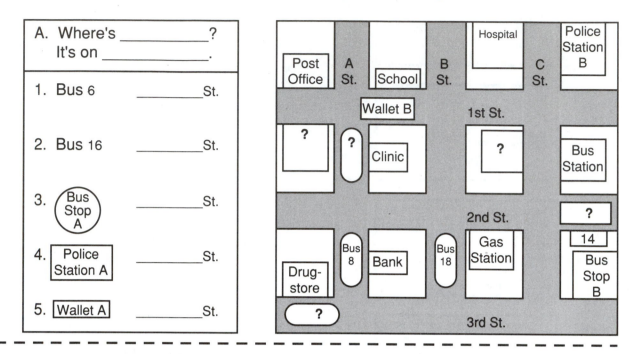

THE MAP GAME. Play with a partner. You are B. Your partner is A.
Listen to your partner's question. Look at your map. Answer the
question. Then look at your box. Where is bus number 8? Ask your
partner. Listen to the answer. Write the street name in your box.

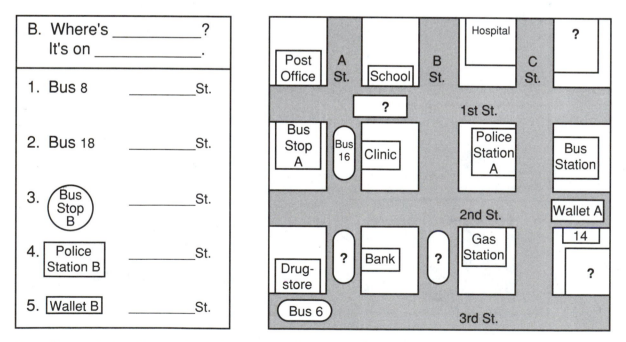

Note: Player A should cover the bottom part of this page. Player B should cover the top part of this
page.

E. Circle T for True or F for False.

1. The woman sees the police station.   T   F

2. The woman gets on the bus.   T   F

3. The woman sees the man's wallet on the street.   T   F

4. The woman wants a new pair of shoes.   T   F

5. An ID is in the man's wallet.   T   F

6. The woman goes into the police station.   T   F

7. The woman buys some new clothes.   T   F

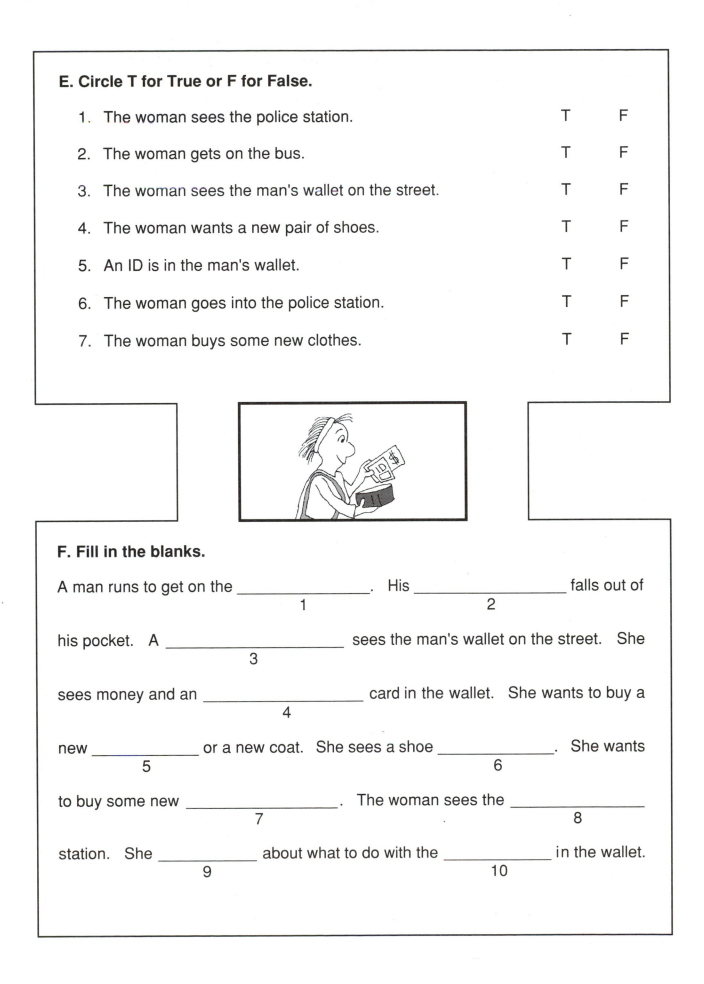

F. Fill in the blanks.

A man runs to get on the _____ . His _____ falls out of
                                    1   2

his pocket. A _____ sees the man's wallet on the street.   She
                          3

sees money and an _____ card in the wallet. She wants to buy a
                                    4

new _____ or a new coat. She sees a shoe _____ . She wants
              5   6

to buy some new _____ .   The woman sees the _____
                          7   8

station. She _____ about what to do with the _____ in the wallet.
                      9   10

G. What do you think? Look at Exercise A. Answer these questions.

What does the woman find? What does she want to do with the money? Does she
need the money? Did anything like this happen to you or anyone you know? What
happened? What should the woman do? What else can she do with the money?

H. Work with your teacher or a partner. Write words you remember from the story.

_____

Now write the story. Use the words to help you.

Teacher's Notes

UNIT I   12 HOURS OLD   Page 1

Topic
Food Storage; Health; Emergencies

Functions
Describing emergency needs; describing physical symptoms; expressing fear/worry; expressing sympathy; offering assistance; requesting assistance.

Situation
A girl has a stomachache after she eats food that hasn't been refrigerated. Her mother takes her to the emergency room.

Cultural Notes
Refrigeration may not be common in many of the students' home countries. Because of this, these cultures are accustomed to buying food for one meal at a time and cooking food only for that meal. In addition, the concept of leftovers may not be common if there are a large number of family members to be fed.

Grammar Focus
Present Continuous Tense; Past Tense; Prepositions of Place

Exercises

A. Talk about the pictures.
1. It's 7:00 P.M. on Monday. A woman cooks dinner.
2. It's 8:00 P.M. The woman and her daughter eat dinner.
3. It's 9:00 P.M. The daughter wants to watch TV.
4. It's 10:30 P.M. The woman tells her daughter to go to bed.
5. It's 3:00 A.M. on Tuesday. The daughter is sleeping. The meat is on the stove.
6. It's 6:30 A.M. The daughter wakes up. The meat is still on the stove.
7. It's 7:00 A.M. The woman gets the meat on the stove.
8. It's 7:00 A.M. The woman takes the pan of meat to the table. Her daughter takes the meat from the pan.
9. It's 11:00 A.M. the daughter has a stomachache.
10. The woman takes her daughter to the emergency room.

Expansion Exercises

Discussion: See Exercise G for discussion questions.

Days of the Week: Using groups of seven different students, give each student a large card with one of the days of the week printed on it. Have students arrange themselves in the correct order. Then have them practice saying each day.

Telling Time: "It's _____ o'clock;...half past _____;... quarter past/to/of _____;..._____thirty; a.m. and p.m." Use a clock with movable hands or give student pairs small clock faces. Call out a time and have students take turns setting the large clock, or their individual clocks, to the time you say.

Past Continuous and Simple Past Tenses: Point to Frames 2, 3, 4, 5, and 6 and have students make sentences using the two tenses with *while* or *when*. For example, "The girl was watching TV when her mother told her to go to bed."

Illness Charades: Teach/review body parts. Then have individual students act out medical problems (for example, holding the stomach to denote a stomachache) and have other students describe the symptoms (for example, "His stomach hurts.").

Map: The mother and daughter live at 11 Apple Road. Have students locate their house and then trace/describe the route that the mother drives to take her daughter to the hospital. (See map on inside front cover.)

B. Number the pictures in order.
Answers: First column: 8, 5, 6, 2, 10. Second column: 9, 1, 7, 3, 4.

C. Match the picture with the sentence.
Answers: 1. c 2. e 3. b 4. f 5. g 6. a 7. d

D. Where do you put it?
Teach/review the names of the items in the left column and the names of the storage places in the right column. Bring in pictures of the items (or the actual items) and large pictures of the four storage areas. Have students place the pictures (or items) next to the appropriate storage area. Then talk about any that might be stored in more than one location (for example, fruit in the refrigerator or on the shelf; fish in the refrigerator or the freezer). Then have students draw a line in their books from each item on the left to the appropriate storage space on the right. They can then describe to each other where they placed the item and why.

Answers: 1. d 2. a or b 3. a or c 4. a 5. c 6. d 7. d 8. b 9. a or b 10. b

Expansion Exercises

Prepositions of Place: Have students practice using *in* and *on* by having them tell where to put the items. For example, "Put the toothpaste in the medicine cabinet. Put the box of tea on the shelf." They can practice with other prepositions of place by following and giving directions to place the items in different areas of the classroom. For example, "under the desk, on top of the table."

Food Products: Bring in food products or their labels which mention proper storage. Have students read the labels and sort by appropriate storage information given (for example, Refrigerate; Refrigerate after opening; Keep cool).

E. True or False
Answers: 1. F 2. T 3. T 4. F 5. F 6. T 7. T

F. Fill in the blanks.
Answers: 1. 7:00 2. dinner 3. daughter 4. bed 5. stove 6. hours 7. daughter 8. takes 9. stomachache 10. emergency

G. What do you think?
Students may want to discuss:

- emergency rooms in U.S. hospitals. (Ask students to make a list of medical emergencies that would require use of the emergency room.)
- students' experiences with medical care in the U.S. including any use of the emergency room, their experiences with doctors and clinics, and their thoughts on the cost of medical care.
- comparison of their own country's medical care system with that of the U.S. (including cost of care, health insurance, and employer's medical coverage plans).

UNIT 2   AT THE SUPERMARKET   Page 7

Topic
Comparison Shopping for Food

Functions
Comparing; describing needs; expressing preferences.

Situation
Two women go shopping with identical lists; one woman compares prices on each item; the other doesn't.

Cultural Notes
In some cultures, food shopping is done in open-air markets and customers bargain for their purchases. In others, stores have fixed prices but only one brand is available. In U.S. supermarkets there is a wide variety of brands with a variety of prices. In order to save money, customers comparison shop by referring to the unit price which is often on the label or posted directly beneath the item on the supermarket shelf. Many stores have a store brand or a generic brand of each food item which is often cheaper than the name brands.

Grammar Focus
Count/Mass Nouns; Comparatives/Superlatives; *both/one/ the other*

Exercises

A. Talk about the pictures.

1. Two women make shopping lists. They are the same.
2. Both women go to the supermarket. One woman has a baby.
3. Both women have shopping baskets. One woman puts her baby in the shopping basket.
4. The two women go to aisle 2.
5. One woman looks at the oil. She doesn't know which one to buy. The other woman takes a box of rice from the shelf.
6. The first woman thinks about how much the oil costs.
7. The women are in aisle 3. One woman looks at the pork. She doesn't know which one to buy. The other woman puts beef in her shopping basket.
8. The first woman thinks about how much the pork costs.
9. Both women go to the checkout counter.
10. One woman pays $34.60. The other woman pays $43.00.

Expansion Exercises

Discussion: See Exercise H for discussion questions.

Supermarket Sections: Bring in food items. Have students categorize the items by sections of the supermar-

ket. For example, dairy, fresh fruits and vegetables, meat, bread.

Container Words: Have students describe the packaging for food items (for example, a carton of milk, a box of cookies, a can of corn, a tube of toothpaste).

Count/Mass Nouns: Teach/review foods that can be counted (five apples, a dozen carrots) and cannot be counted (some fruit, a lot of hamburger, a little fish) by putting out pictures of various items and having students divide them into the two groups. Practice using *how many/how much* questions for quantities by using the pictures for a role-play. Students take turns being the salespeople and customers and asking each other questions like: "How much broccoli do you want? How many bananas do you want?" Students respond with a number (for example, five) or a quantity (for example, a lot, a few, a little).

Both, One, the Other: Because the two women do similar as well as different things in the story, students can focus on using *both* as well as *one* and *the other* when they tell the story. To practice this distinction, ask students to make a list of their favorite things, for example, foods/colors/famous people/jobs they want. Divide students into pairs and have them compare their lists. Then have pairs report to the class their preferences by saying: "Both of us like _____. But only one of us likes _____ and the other likes _____."

Map: The supermarket is on Orange Street. One of the women lives at 21 Bank Street. Have students locate the house and then trace/describe the route she takes from her home to the supermarket. (See map on inside front cover.)

B. Number the pictures in order.
Answers: First column: 3, 9, 1, 8, 6.   Second column: 5, 10, 2, 7, 4.

C. Match the picture with the sentence.
Answers: 1. c 2. e 3. f 4. a 5. g 6. b 7. d

D. Listen to the teacher.
Read the script and have students circle the price they hear. Remind students that they do not need to understand every word, only the prices. If students are very low-level, read only the prices, for example, "Number one, ninety eight cents." Script:

1. The hamburger meat costs ninety eight cents a pound.
2. This oil is expensive. It's thirteen dollars and one cent a gallon.
3. Prices are really going up. The dish detergent now costs one dollar and eighty nine cents.
4. This candy bar is on sale for forty one cents.
5. A gallon of milk costs two dollars and eighty cents at my neighborhood store.
6. During the sale you can buy a case of paper towels for four dollars and thirty cents.
7. Apples are in season. They're only fifity four cents a pound.

Answers: 1. c 2. b 3. b 4. b 5. c 6. b 7. a

E. Choose the best buy.
Bring in labels from food items that have unit prices on them (for example, meat items) or attach unit price labels to pictures of food items. Have students practice reading the unit price, the net weight, and the total price. If possible, bring in the same items with different unit prices and have students tell you which are the best deals. Then have

students read the labels in Exercise E and choose which items they would buy. Students will probably choose the cheapest, but they may choose a more expensive unit price because they don't want such a large quantity or because they think the quality may be better.

Expansion Exercises

Comparatives/Superlatives: Using the items in the activity, have students use comparatives and superlatives to talk about the prices. For example, "Rice a is cheaper than Rice b; Rice c is the most expensive."

Food Items/Prices: Bring in supermarket flyers. Give students a handout with questions (for example, "How much are the bananas? What brand of laundry detergent is on sale?") and have them work in pairs to answer the questions.

Shopping List: Divide students into groups of three. Have students make a shopping list of food their group will need to prepare breakfast, lunch, and dinner tomorrow. After they have made a shopping list of food for the next three meals, have them go to a supermarket and figure out what products they should buy in order to save the most money.

Supermarket Role-Play: Set up the classroom to look like the aisles in a supermarket. Put food pictures in different locations. Have at least two of each food item. Put different price tags on each item. Prices can be written as unit prices. Give students shopping lists in pairs. Have the pairs choose the cheapest item by comparing prices. Then have the students add up their total shopping bill and compare it with the other groups.

F. True or False
Answers: 1. F 2. T 3. T 4. F 5. T 6. T 7. F

G. Fill in the blanks.
Answers: 1. supermarket 2. baby 3. go 4. thinks 5. oil 6. aisle 7. pork 8. puts 9. women 10. pays

H. What do you think?
Students may want to discuss:

- ways of saving money when shopping for food (for example, buying in bulk; not shopping when hungry; not buying junk food; buying generic brands; using coupons).

- shopping at a large supermarket versus a neighborhood convenience store.

- shopping in farmers' markets.

- bargaining for food versus fixed prices.

UNIT 3   D3 TO E4   Page 13

Topic
Employer/Employee Relationships; On-the-Job Responsibilities

Functions
Asking for information; clarifying, following directions; instructing.

Situation
A woman supervisor explains to an employee how to connect a group of wires but one of her instructions is wrong. Although the man has questions about her instructions, he does not challenge her.

Cultural Notes
In some cultures, it is considered impolite to question a person in a supervisory position, even to confirm or clarify information. In the U.S., employers expect employees to confirm or clarify. For many men new to the U.S., having a woman as a supervisor will be unusual.

Grammar Focus
Present Continuous Tense

Exercises

A. Talk about the pictures.

1. A (woman) supervisor says, "D1 to E5."
2. A man connects D1 to E5.
3. The (woman) supervisor says, "D2 to E1."
4. The man connects D2 to E1.
5. The (woman) supervisor says, "D5 to E4."
6. The man connects D5 to E4.
7. The (woman) supervisor says, "D3 to E4."
8. The man thinks, "E4?" He puts the wires together. (He connects D3 to E4.)
9. The (woman) supervisor sees the problem. (The supervisor is surprised.)
10. There's a fire.

Expansion Exercises

Discussion: See Exercise H for discussion questions.

Correcting: Have students role-play appropriate ways to correct or question others, including a person in authority, a child, a work colleague, a friend, someone much older.

Pronunciation: Work with students on numbers and letters which are difficult to pronounce. For example, students could practice distinguishing between *fifty* and *fifteen*, *thirty* and *thirteen*. They might also practice stressing ending consonant sounds (for example, the *v* sound in *five*).

Present Continuous Tense: Have students take the role of the supervisor and explain to the class the sequence of steps in the story as they are connecting numbers on a grid. For example, "I'm connecting D1 to E5. Now I'm connecting D2 to E1."

Map: The man works at PKW Factory and he lives at 23 Apple Road. Have students trace/describe his route from his home to his job. Then trace the route the fire department would take to get to the PKW Factory. (See map on inside front cover.)

B. Number the pictures in order.
Answers: First column: 9, 2, 7, 6, 1.   Second column: 3, 5, 8, 10, 4.

C. Match the picture with the sentence.
Answers: 1. c 2. e 3. a 4. g 5. d 6. b 7. f

D. Listen to the teacher.
Draw the example box on the board. Read the letter/number combinations in each column out loud to the students while pointing to each one. (D1, D2, D3, etc.) Then ask individual students to come to the board and draw a line to connect the combinations that you read orally. ("D1 to E5; D3 to E4," etc.). After students have practiced in the large group, read the script below and have students connect the combinations in their books by drawing a line. This exercise can be done more than once by changing the connections.

Script:

1. D1 to E5
2. B5 to G3
3. A2 to C7
4. E1 to F6
5. C5 to J5
6. F7 to K11

Expansion Exercises

Dictation: Read a list of letter/number combinations aloud to students. Students write the correct combinations.

Silent Dictation: Write numbers (for example, 6, 15, 5) on the board. Students then write out the number words (six, fifteen, five) on their paper.

E. The Map

Draw the map from page 16 on the board or on a large sheet of paper which can be posted in front of the class. Have students do the exercise orally as they look at the board map. Then have the students individually fill in the answers in the exercise in their books.
Answers: 1. C4 2. A3 3. B1 4. C2 5. B2 6. B3 7. A2 8. C1 9. A1

Expansion Exercises

Giving Directions: Using the map in Exercise E, have students in pairs give each other directions to certain buildings. Students sit back to back with the map in front of each one. Student A silently chooses a building and tells Student B where it is using the letter/number combination. Student B must tell student A the name of the building.

Numbers: Write letter/number combinations on the board. Divide the class into two teams. The teams line up in front of the board. Call out a combinations. One member from each team runs to the board and circles the combination read. The first student to circle the correct combination gets a point for his team.

F. True or False
Answers: 1. T 2. T 3. T 4. T 5. F 6. F 7. F

G. Fill in the blanks.
Answers: 1. man 2. supervisor/woman 3. D1 4. puts/connects 5. Connect 6. together 7. He 8. says 9. wires 10. fire/explosion

H. What do you think?
Students may want to discuss:

■ appropriate ways of correcting or questioning a person in authority.

■ possible consequences of correcting or questioning a person in authority.

■ feelings about women as supervisors.

UNIT 4   THE DENTIST   Page 19
Topic
Health Care; Dental Insurance; Emergencies

Functions
Asking for help; asking for medical information; describing a problem; expressing fear; expressing pain; giving advice; giving personal information.

Situation
A man has a tooth removed at a dental clinic. He doesn't have insurance.

Cultural Notes
Students from other countries may arrive in the U.S. with dental problems requiring extensive work. Dental care is much more sophisticated and expensive in the U.S. than in some developing countries or in countries with socialized medical care. In many countries teeth are often removed rather than repaired; in the U.S. dentists try to save a tooth, but sometimes repair is impossible because of extensive damage. Dental care in the U.S. is often not covered under employers' insurance programs.

Grammar Focus
Past Tense of Regular and Irregular Verbs; Reported Speech; Future Tense

Exercises

A. Talk about the pictures.
1. A man has a toothache.
2. The man goes to the dental clinic.
3. The dentist says, "Sit down in the chair."
4. The dentist looks in the man's mouth.
5. The dentist takes an x-ray.
6. The dentist gives the man an injection.
7. The dentist pulls the man's tooth. The man spits in the sink.
8. The dentist holds the man's tooth.
9. The man says, "Thank you."
10. The nurse asks, "Do you have insurance?" The man says, "No."

Expansion Exercises

Discussion: See Exercise G for discussion questions.

Dental Care: Bring in items for dental care such as a toothbrush, toothpaste, dental floss. Also, have students identify food which is healthy for teeth. Bring in pictures of different food items (for example, carrots, apples, celery, candy bars, gum, soda) and have students divide food into healthy and unhealthy foods.

Past Tense: Have students tell the story in the past tense as if they were the man with the toothache and describing to a friend what happened. Students will practice using common regular and irregular past tense verbs.

Reported Speech: Give students the quotation from the story: The man said, "I don't have insurance." Have them convert the quotation to reported speech: "The man said that he didn't have insurance." Then give the students other quotations, perhaps from previous picture stories the class has read, and have them change these quotations to reported speech.

Future Tense: Have students take the role of the dentist and practice describing to the patient what he'll do. For example, "First I'll look at your tooth. Then I'll take an x-ray. After that I'll give you an injection and then I'll pull your tooth."

Map: The dentist's office is located in the California Street Clinic building. The man lives at 22 1st Street. Have students locate the clinic and the man's home and then trace/describe the route he takes from his home to the dental clinic. (See map on inside front cover.)

B. Number the pictures in order.
Answers: First column: 9, 4, 8, 3, 1.   Second column: 6, 7, 10, 2, 5.

C. Match the picture with the sentence.
Answers: 1. c 2. d 3. a 4. g 5. b 6. e 7. f

D. Listen to the teacher.
Write a sample appointment card on the chalkboard. Read aloud number 1 from the script below and have students help you fill in the card on the board. Then read aloud the information below for each card. Students write the correct information in their texts.
Script:

1. Mr. E. Lee has an appointment on Friday, September 12th, at 1:00 P.M.
2. Mrs. B. Brown has an appointment on the morning of August 7th at 9:30. That's a Monday.
3. Mr. P. Brown can see the doctor at 11:45 A.M. on Wednesday, the 6th of January.
4. Your daughter is scheduled to see the doctor on Tuesday, May 22nd, at 3:15 P.M.
5. You have an appointment to see the doctor on the 1st of March at 2:30 P.M. That's a Thursday.
6. The doctor can see your mother on Friday, December 13th at 10:00 in the morning.

Expansion Exercises

Appointment Cards: Make simple appointment cards (similar to the ones in Exercise D) that include date and time of appointment. Give each student one card, ask several students to tell you the day, date, and time of the appointment and the name and location of the dentist. Then have them ask each other the questions in pairs or dictate the information on their card to a partner. Partners can write the information onto a blank appointment card.

Using a Telephone: To simulate using a telephone, have students practice writing down the above information without being able to see you as you read. Then have them ask for clarification if they didn't understand. Finally, have students check what they have recorded with a partner and with the teacher if there is disagreement.

E. True or False
Answers: 1. T 2. F 3. F 4. F 5. T 6. T 7. T

F. Fill in the blanks.
Answers: 1. toothache 2. clinic 3. Sit 4. chair 5. mouth 6. dentist 7. injection 8. pulls 9. Thank 10. have

G. What do you think?
Students may want to discuss:

- good and bad tooth care habits including eating fruits and vegetables rather than candy for snacks; brushing and flossing teeth; visiting the dentist regularly.
- ways of repairing damaged teeth rather than removing them.
- ways to ask a dentist about alternatives to tooth removal.
- the cost of dental care and dental insurance.

UNIT 5   DO NOT TOUCH   Page 25
Topic
Workplace Safety; On-the-Job Responsibilities

Functions
Following directions; reading signs/symbols.

Situation
A man gets in trouble when he doesn't read important signs in the workplace.

Cultural Notes
In non-industrial societies literacy is not as essential as it is in the U.S. workplace. The ability to read basic safety signs is assumed in the U.S. and is necessary for keeping a job and staying safe.

Grammar Focus
Imperatives

Exercises

A. Talk about the pictures.

1. A man looks at the door of room number 4. There is a DO NOT ENTER sign beside the door.
2. The man opens the door.
3. The man walks down the hall. There is a KEEP CLOSED sign on the door of room number 5.
4. The man walks past room number 6. There is a KEEP OUT sign on the door.
5. The man opens the door to room number 7. The sign says AUTHORIZED PERSONNEL ONLY. There is a NO SMOKING sign on the wall.
6. The man sees a machine. The sign on the machine says DO NOT TOUCH. There is a DANGER sign on the wall.
7. The man wants to push the button on the machine.
8. The man looks around.
9. The man pushes the button.
10. The machine falls on the man.

Expansion Exercises

Discussion: See Exercise H for discussion questions.

Imperatives: Use the picture story for practice with affirmative and negative imperatives. Have students follow instructions related to the picture story. For example "Look at the sign. Go through the door. Touch the button. Don't touch the button." Then have students give instructions to each other.

Map: The man works at the PKW Factory. Have students trace/describe the route he takes everyday to work from his apartment in KC Apartments. Also have them find the route the ambulance will take from the PKW Factory to the hospital. (See map on inside front cover.)

B. Number the pictures in order.
Answers: First column: 2, 4, 8, 6, 7.   Second column: 10, 3, 5, 9, 1.

C. Match the picture with the sentence.
Answers: 1. c 2. f 3. a 4. g 5. b 6. e 7. d

D. Match the picture with the word.
Teach the sight words by showing large visuals of the symbols or signs and large word cards of the vocabulary. OR First do the exercise orally with the whole class.
Answers: 1. b 2. h 3. g 4. c 5. d 6. e 7. f 8. a

Expansion Exercises

Emergency Signs: Write the emergency "signs" from Exercise D randomly on the board. (Add any other signs that seem appropriate.) Divide the class into two teams. Read one of the signs aloud. One student from each team runs up to the board and touches the correct "sign." The first one to touch it wins. OR Hold up a picture which illustrates the meaning of the sign (without talking) and have students find the correct "sign" on the board.

Matching: Prepare cards with common workplace safety signs written on them. For example, DO NOT ENTER, NO SMOKING. Also prepare cards illustrating the meaning of each sign. Place the cards face down. Have students take turns turning over two cards at a time to try and make a match.

E. Three in a Row
Have students play the game. (See Introduction, Play the Game, page ix.)

F. True or False
Answers: 1. T 2. F 3. T 4. F 5. T 6. F 7. F

G. Fill in the blanks.
Answers: 1. ENTER 2. door 3. hall 4. KEEP 5. OUT 6. room 7. machine 8. button 9. pushes 10. drops/falls

H. What do you think?
Students may want to discuss:

- the importance of literacy skills in the workplace.

- where to go in your community to get help if you can't read.

- the dangers and consequences of not following directions.

UNIT 6   THE HEATER   Page 31
Topic
Safety in the Home

Functions
Advising; describing a physical state; discussing a problem; expressing a need; reporting an emergency.

Situation
A man buys a new heater because his apartment is too cold. He puts his new heater too close to his bed and causes a fire.

Cultural Notes
Students from warm climates will not be accustomed to winters in the U.S. They may have had no experience with central heating systems or with electrical space heaters. They may also live in older, uninsulated apartments that are difficult to heat. Putting a space heater too close to flammable objects may cause a fire.

Grammar Focus
It's + Adjective; Comparatives/Superlatives; Intensifiers: *too/enough/so/such*

Exercises
A. Talk about the pictures.

1. A man and a woman are cold.
2. The man puts on his coat.
3. The man goes to CJ Department Store.
4. The man buys a heater. He pays $38.50.
5. The man leaves the department store.
6. The man takes the heater into the bedroom.

7. The man plugs in the heater.
8. The man puts the heater next to the bed.
9. The heater is on. The man and woman are asleep.
10. There is a fire.

Expansion Exercises

Discussion: See Exercise H for discussion questions.

Clothing Match: Bring in winter clothing items or pictures and have students identify them (for example, scarf, hat, mittens, gloves, cap, overcoat, jacket). Have students match word cards with pictures of clothing items.

Emergency Phone Calls: Have students practice making emergency phone calls with a toy phone to report a fire, a sick child, an injured person, a car accident, a robbery.

Map: The couple lives at 17 Coffee Avenue. Have students locate their house on the map. Ask students to find the CJ Department Store. Have students trace/describe the route that the man takes to buy the heater. Have students find the fire department and trace/describe the shortest route that the fire engine will take to get to their home. (See map on inside front cover.)

B. Number the pictures in order.
Answers: First column: 2, 9, 3, 10, 7. Second column: 4, 6, 1, 5, 8.

C. Match the picture with the sentence.
Answers: 1. c 2. d 3. g 4. e 5. b 6. a 7. f

D. Listen to the teacher.
Say one temperature from each column. Students circle the correct letter. The exercise can be done several times if students write in pencil then erase. The script below is only a suggestion.
Script:

1. It's 18°.
2. It's 23°.
3. It's 60°.
4. It's 64°.
5. It's 17°.

E. Listen to the teacher.
Read the example statements below. Have students listen for the correct temperature, then fill in the thermometer to the correct number. It is not necessary for them to understand all the words.
Script:

1. "It's nice out. I think it's 70 degrees."
2. "Can you believe how hot it is? It must be 100 degrees!"
3. "You'll need a jacket. It's about 55 degrees out."
4. "Oh! It's freezing! It's only 10 degrees!"
5. "It's pretty cold...exactly 32 degrees!"
6. "You'll need at least a sweater. It's about 60 degrees."
7. "Put on your heavy coat and boots. It's snowing and it's only 20 degrees."
8. "The children should not go outside. It's 5 degrees out!"
9. "Make sure you drink lots of water. It's hot...90 degrees!"
10. "Put on your hat. It's 40 degrees out."

Expansion Exercises

Weather Terms: Teach weather terms (hot, cold, rainy, sunny, etc.). Have an ongoing daily discussion of the weather to reinforce terms. Low-level students can put pictures of current weather conditions on a chart every day and then match these pictures to the appropriate words.

Weather Charts: Have students read newspaper weather reports or a weather map and answer prepared questions about the weather. (For example, "What was the high temperature in New York yesterday? Will it rain tomorrow?")

It's + Adjective: For example, "It's cold." Have students describe the weather daily using the expression "It's _____."

Comparatives and Superlatives: For example, "It's colder than yesterday. 50 degrees is colder than 60 degrees. It's the hottest day of the year." Have students look at the thermometers after they have completed the listening exercises and compare two of the temperatures ("Seventy degrees is hotter than twenty degrees.") or three or more of the temperatures ("One hundred degrees is the hottest temperature.").

So/Such and Too/Enough: For example, "It's so cold. It's too hot to play outside. It's such a hot day that I can't play outside. It's hot enough to fry an egg." Have students use these intensifiers to describe the temperatures in Exercise E.

F. True or False
Answers: 1. T 2. F 3. T 4. T 5. T 6. F 7. F

G. Fill in the blanks.
Answers: 1. woman 2. coat 3. goes 4. buys 5. store 6. heater 7. plugs 8. puts 9. bed 10. man

H. What do you think?
Students may want to discuss:

- ways to keep warm in a cold climate. Students might mention turning up the heat (which can lead to a discussion of cost); wearing more clothes (a discussion of losing heat through the top of the head); weatherproofing the house.

- what to do if the landlord does not provide adequate heat (how to make a phone call to the landlord to request more heat; how to work with tenants' rights groups or other available social services; a discussion of tenants' and landlords' responsibilities).

UNIT 7   HOUSE ON FIRE   Page 37

Topic
Household Safety; Emergencies

Functions
Expressing emotions; making choices; reporting an emergency.

Situation
A man takes three things with him (his cat, his ID, and his address book) when his house catches on fire.

Cultural Notes
What a person saves in a disaster may differ greatly from culture to culture.

In most Western countries, there is an emergency number to use in case of an accident, a medical emergency, or a fire (911 is the emergency number in larger cities in the U.S.). Some students will be from cultures where there are no telephones, and even for those who are familiar with the use of telephones, the concept of a telephone number to call in an emergency is not usual.

Grammar Focus
Imperatives; Past and Past Continuous Tenses; Separable Phrasal (two-word) Verbs; Ordinal/Cardinal Numbers

Exercises

A. Talk about the pictures.

1. A man sleeps upstairs.
2. The man wakes up and smells smoke.
3. The man sees a fire and yells, "Fire!"
4. The man gets out of bed. He looks out the window.
5. The man runs downstairs.
6. The man picks up his cat.
7. The man picks up his ID card.
8. The man picks up his address book.
9. The man drops everything out the window.
10. The man climbs out the window.

Expansion Exercises

Discussion: See Exercise H for discussion questions.

Emergency Phone Calls: Give students 3x5 cards with an emergency situation drawn or written on each card. Have the student read the situation and then call to report the emergency. The student can choose the appropriate number from a list of emergency numbers (fire, police, ambulance, poison center) written on the blackboard. The teacher or a more advanced student can take the role of the operator.

Imperatives: Have students give each other commands to act out the sequence of actions in the story. For example, "Wake up. Get up. Look out the window. Run downstairs," etc.

Past and Past Continuous Tenses: Students take the role of a TV reporter who is reporting what happened at the scene of a fire a few hours before. For example, "A man was sleeping upstairs when he woke up and smelled smoke."

Separable Phrasal (two-word) Verbs: Point out the two phrasal verbs *wake up* and *get up* from the story and show the students that they can say: "Wake the man up." or "Wake up the man." Teach/review other phrasal verbs that can be separated. Play a matching game with the phrasal verb on one card and the definition on another. Then have students ask each other questions using common phrasal verbs.

Map: The man lives in J's Apartments. Have students trace/describe the route from the fire station to his apartment building.

B. Number the pictures in order.
Answers: First column: 4, 9, 10, 1, 6. Second column: 2, 5, 7, 8, 3.

C. Match the picture with the sentence.
Answers: 1. c 2. f 3. b 4. g 5. a 6. e 7. d

D. What do you save?
Review the vocabulary in the pictures (TV; money; address book; baby/child; English book; ID card; clothes; cat (pets); photo album; radio/cassette recorder). Ask students to think about which items are most important to them. Then have them put a number in each of the boxes above the pictures. Number 1 is the most important to them and number 10 is the least important. After students have ordered the pictures, ask them if there are items they would save that are not in these pictures.

E. Listen to the teacher.

Teach/review the names of the three emergency services by showing pictures to match to the words or asking students for definitions. Practice reading addresses using ordinal and cardinal numbers. Then practice reading telephone numbers, pausing between the third and the fourth numbers. Point out to students that when they call an emergency service they will need to give the nature of the emergency, the address where the service should go, and the telephone number from which they are calling.

Then read the script as if you are calling from the scene of an emergency. You may want to speak rapidly or excitedly as you might in an emergency. Students circle the information they hear. You may need to repeat each item.
Script:

1. Help! Fire department! There's a fire at 10 9th Street. My phone number is 561-6535.
2. Is this the hospital? There's been an accident at 30 L Street. Please send an ambulance. My number is 235-4890.
3. Police! Come quickly. I've been robbed. My address is 4 1st Street. My phone number is 381-6767.
4. My baby drank poison! I need an ambulance quickly. Come to 17 F Street. My phone number is 739-0040.
5. There's a car on fire at 20 2nd Street. Send the fire department immediately. My number is 484-4800.

Answers: 1. a, c, b 2. a, a, c 3. a, c, a 4. b, b, c
5. b, b, c

Expansion Exercises

Ordinal Numbers: Write ordinal and cardinal numbers 1 through 10 on the blackboard in random order. Call out an ordinal number. Have students take turns going to the board, finding and circling the number they hear. Then ask the students to give the equivalent cardinal number. Make this activity into a game with two teams. One student from each team runs to the board; the first student to circle the number that the teacher calls, gets a point for his team. Students can then practice the ordinal and cardinal numbers by giving their own street addresses or by reading street addresses similar to the ones in Exercise E that the teacher has written on index cards.

Pronunciation—Letters of the Alphabet: Although students may be familiar with the Roman alphabet, they may pronounce the letters as they would in their own language. This could cause problems in reporting an emergency when they need to give or spell a street address. Students can practice by circling the letter you say: for example, E, I, A.

F. True or False
Answers: 1. T 2. F 3. T 4. T 5. F 6. T 7. T

G. Fill in the blanks.
Answers: 1. wakes 2. smells 3. fire 4. gets 5. downstairs
6. picks 7. ID 8. address 9. drops 10. window

H. What do you think?
Students may want to discuss:

- what to save during an emergency.
- what to do if there is a fire in one's house/apartment.
- whether or not to use the telephone or to call from a neighbor's house.

- how to keep a fire from starting.
- the responsibilities of a landlord or tenant to make an apartment safe from fires.

UNIT 8   THE JOB INTERVIEW   Page 43
Topic
Looking for a Job; Male-Female Roles/Relationships; Employer/Employee Relationships

Functions
Expressing emotions; getting information; responding to questions; stating qualifications.

Situation
A man and a woman both apply for jobs. The woman gets a job but the man doesn't.

Cultural Notes
In many of the students' cultures, it is not common for the woman to work outside the home. The main source of income usually comes from the husband. It will be surprising to some students to consider that the woman may be more employable than the man and that in some cases the woman may be supporting the family.

Grammar Focus
Verb: *to be*; Pronouns; WH Questions; Present Perfect Tense

Exercises

A. Talk about the pictures.

1. A man and a woman look in the newspaper for jobs.
2. The man and the woman look at the ads for two jobs. The woman looks at an ad for G and D Grocery. The man looks at an ad for M and N Grocery.
3. The woman goes to the office at G and D Grocery. The man goes to the office at M and N Grocery.
4. The man and the woman both say, "I want a job."
5. The employers give the man and the woman job applications.
6. The man and the woman fill out job applications.
7. The man and the woman give the employers their job applications.
8. The employers ask the man and the woman questions. The man and the woman ask the employers questions.
9. The employer says to the woman, "You can start work on Monday." The employer calls the man at home and says, "Sorry, we don't have a job for you."
10. The woman starts work as a cashier on Monday. The man looks in the newspaper again for a job.

Expansion Exercises

Discussion: See Exercise H for discussion questions.

Occupations/To Be: Teach the names of different jobs. Ask students what jobs the man and the woman are applying for. Ask them to identify the jobs that might be available in this kind of company. Ask students what jobs they have. Show pictures of common occupations and have students point to and/or name their job or one they would like to have. Have students focus on the verb *to be* in present and past tenses as they ask questions about and describe their current and past jobs and those of their classmates. For example, "I was a mechanic in Vietnam."

Pronouns: Have students tell the story using personal pronouns in place of the nouns: man, woman, employer.

Job Rejection Role-Plays: Have students develop a conversation between the man and woman when the woman comes home with a job and the man doesn't.

Map: The man and woman live next to the bus station on 3rd Street. Ask students to find their house and trace/describe the route that they take to the job sites for interviews. (See map on inside front cover.)

B. Number the pictures in order.
Answers: First column: 6, 2, 3, 1, 8.   Second column: 4, 9, 5, 10, 7.

C. Match the picture with the sentence.
Answers: 1. c 2. d 3. g 4. f 5. a 6. e 7. b

D. and E. Job Application
Teach the job application vocabulary by writing the words in Exercise D on index cards. Students take turns choosing cards and responding to words written on the cards with personal information. For example, a student chooses the card *area code* and responds "802." Then have one student choose a card and ask another student a question related to the word on the card. For example, *Employment:* "What was your last job?" or *Place:* "Where did you work?"

More advanced students can think of additional words that are common on job applications and write them on index cards to play as above. Then the students fill out the job application form in the book.

Expansion Exercises

Pair Interviews/ WH questions: 1. After students have filled out the application form, divide them into two groups. One group develops a list of questions an employer might ask in an interview. The other group makes a list of questions an applicant might ask. The two groups look at both lists and identify the questions most likely and least likely to be asked. Students can then do pair interviews. 2. Divide students into pairs. Give each student a blank copy of the job application form. Students ask their partners questions in turn in order to fill out the application form based on their partners' answers (for example, NAME: "What's your name?").

Job Interview Role-Play/Present Perfect: Do a simulated job interview with students. Students can prepare by filling out a job application or preparing a simple resume. They then present the job application/resume to the employer (the teacher or another person from outside the class) and go through an interview process. Focus on "How long have you...?" and "Have you ever ...?" questions to help students practice understanding and responding to questions in the present perfect tense.

Classified Ads: Bring in help wanted ads from newspapers. Give pairs of students an ad and a list of questions to answer about the ad. For example, "What are the qualifications? What is the salary? How do you respond to the ad" (send a resume, call for an appointment, etc.)? Have pairs answer the questions and then explain the job to a second pair.

F. True or False
Answers: 1. F 2. T 3. T 4. T 5. F 6. F 7. F

G. Fill in the blanks.
Answers: 1. job 2. husband 3. ad 4. Grocery 5. asked 6. Monday 7. get 8. interview 9. newspaper 10. job

H. What do you think?
Students may want to discuss:

- feelings about not getting accepted for a job that you want.

- what happens when a traditional husband is supported by his wife.

- how childcare will be handled if the woman is working.

- possible reasons why the woman was hired and not the man.

UNIT 9   NO EXIT   Page 49

Topic
Transportation Safety; Traffic Signs; Medical Care; Emergencies

Functions
Expressing pain; expressing surprise; giving personal information; reading signs and symbols; reporting/describing an accident.

Situtation
Two people have an automobile accident when one of them doesn't read a NO EXIT sign. After a stay in a hospital, the injured man has another accident when he doesn't read a DON'T WALK sign.

Cultural Notes
In other countries, transportation rules, behaviors, and expectations may be different from those in the U.S. Students need to know it is everyone's responsibility to be aware of safety rules. Transportation safety depends on the ability of both drivers and pedestrians to read and respond appropriately to traffic signs and signals.

Grammar Focus
Past and Future Tenses

Exercises

A. Talk about the pictures.

1. Two cars are at an intersection. One car is going the wrong way. One sign says DO NOT ENTER. The other sign says NO EXIT.
2. The two cars have an accident.
3. A woman sees the accident. She calls an ambulance (911).
4. The ambulance arrives. The ambulance driver puts the man in the ambulance.
5. The ambulance takes the man to the emergency room at the hospital.
6. It's Tuesday. The man is in room 119. He is in bed.
7. It's Friday. A nurse is standing beside the bed. She says, "You're OK."
8. It's Saturday. The man gets his hospital bill. It's $5760. (He owes a lot of money.)
9. The man is on the sidewalk. The sign says DON'T WALK.
10. The man crosses the street. A car hits him.

Discussion: See Exercise H for discussion questions.

Past Tense: Have students tell the story in the past tense so they can practice using common regular and irregular past tense verbs. Students can take the role of a reporter describing the traffic accidents.

Future Tense: Have students practice describing events that are about to happen using the future tense with *going to* or *about to.* For example, in Frame 8: "The man is about to pay his bill."

Emergency Phone Calls: Have students work in pairs to create the conversation between the woman who reports the accident and the 911 operator. The teacher or an advanced student can take the role of the operator.

Hospital Vocabulary: Have students share experiences they have had in hospitals. Make a list of common vocabulary and phrases a patient should understand and be able to respond to.

Map: The first accident happens at North High School. The second accident happens in front of the hospital. Have students trace and describe the route between the two. (See map on inside front cover.)

B. Number the pictures in order.
Answers: First column: 6, 2, 3, 9, 7. Second column: 10, 5, 4, 8, 1.

C. Match the picture with the sentence.
Answers: 1. c 2. e 3. a 4. f 5. d 6. b 7. g

D. Match the picture with the word.
Teach the sight words by showing large visuals of the symbols or signs and large word cards of the vocabulary. OR First do the exercise orally with the whole class.
Answers: 1. b 2. c 3. e 4. g 5. a 6. h 7. d 8. f

Expansion Exercise

Transportation Signs and Symbols: Bring in pictures of common transportation signs and symbols or draw them on the board. Have students identify them and indicate verbally or with actions what they should do when they see the sign or symbol.

E. Three in a Row
Have students play the game. (See Introduction, Play the Game, page ix.)

F. True or False
Answers: 1. T 2. F 3. T 4. F 5. T 6. T 7. F

G. Fill in the blanks.
Answers: 1. NOT 2. EXIT 3. accident 4. calls 5. ambulance 6. emergency 7. owes 8. hospital 9. see(read) 10. WALK

H. What do you think?
Students may want to discuss:

- expectations of Americans regarding driving in the U.S.

- the responsibilities of pedestrians and drivers.

- transportation rules that are different from those students are accustomed to.

- the expense of a hospital stay in the U.S.

- what a person can do if he or she cannot read.

UNIT 10   OK, NO JOB   Page 55
Topic
Employer/Employee Relationships; Male/Female Roles/ Relationships; Workplace Rules and Policies

Functions
Expressing desire; expressing displeasure; instructing/ commanding.

Situation
A male manager calls a female employee into his office. When she refuses to kiss him, he threatens to fire her.

Cultural Notes
This story presents an abuse of authority and position. Men (or women) are not entitled to use their positions to seek personal or sexual favors from their employees. Women employees need to know they do not have to become intimately involved with their employers or co-workers. Women who are pressured or threatened with the loss of their jobs should contact their union or seek legal counsel.

Grammar Focus
Past Continuous and Past Tenses; Reported Speech

Exercises

A. Talk about the pictures.

1. A woman is working (at her desk) in an office.
2. Her boss calls her into his office. He points inside the office.
3. She asks, "What?" He says, "Come here."
4. She goes into his office. He pinches her as she walks by. She is surprised.
5. He sits down on the couch. He says, "Come here."
6. She sits down. She asks, "What do you want."
7. He tries to kiss her. She says, "No."
8. He asks, "Do you like your job?" She says, "Yes."
9. He asks, "Can I kiss you?" She says, "No."
10. He says, "OK, no job."

Expansion Exercises

Discussion: See Exercise G for discussion questions.

Past Continuous with Simple Past: Have the students practice combining sentences from the story using the two tenses. For example, "The woman was sitting on the couch when her boss tried to kiss her."

Reported Speech: More advanced students can retell the story from the woman's point of view and then from the man's point of view. For example, "I asked what he wanted and he asked if I liked my job."

Map: This story takes place at the TV station. Have students find it on the map. (See map on inside front cover.)

B. Number the pictures in order.
Answers: First column: 9, 10, 3, 1, 6. Second column: 4, 2, 8, 5, 7.

C. Match the picture with the sentence.
Answers: 1. c 2. f 3. b 4. d 5. a 6. e 7. g

D. Check the activities that are OK.
Teach/review the vocabulary that describes the actions shown in pictures 1 through 9. Then have students look at the pictures in the column on the left and put a check

to indicate if the activities that are pictured are OK to do in the U.S. or in their country. Have students share their answers and discuss any differences and the implications of the actions both in the U.S. and in their own countries.

E. True or False
Answers: 1. T 2. F 3. T 4. T 5. F 6. T 7. T

F. Fill in the blanks.
Answers: 1. sits 2. man (manager) 3. woman 4. office 5. pinches 6. surprised 7. couch (sofa) 8. kiss 9. you 10. job

G. What do you think?
Students may want to discuss:

- behaviors that qualify as on-the-job harassment.

- measures a person can take to avoid the behaviors or deal with them when they happen.

UNIT 11   ONE HOUR   Page 61

Topic
On-the-Job Responsibilities/Expectations; Employer/Employee Relationships

Functions
Expressing confusion; expressing dissatisfaction; instructing; responding to discipline/reprimands.

Situation
A man is told to assemble a chair in one hour. When he can't find a screwdriver, he waits for his supervisor to come back. The supervisor is angry because the chair is not finished.

Cultural Notes
Employers expect employees to do tasks they are assigned. This involves asking for clarification if a task isn't clear; asking for help if a task is too difficult; requesting equipment or materials if/when they're needed; reporting problems. The person in this story decides to wait rather than report the problem to his boss or go get a screwdriver himself. In the supervisor's eyes, the employee does not show any initiative.

Grammar Focus
Imperatives

Exercises

A. Talk about the pictures.

1. A supervisor shows a picture of a chair to an employee. He says, "Make this in one hour." The man says, "OK."
2. The supervisor gives a box (of materials) to the man.
3. The man opens the box.
4. He holds a wrench. He takes pieces of the chair out of the box.
5. He looks at the tools.
6. The man can't find a screwdriver. He asks, "Where is the screwdriver?"
7. He says, "There's no screwdriver."
8. It is 1:30 P.M. The man looks at his watch.
9. The supervisor returns at 2:00. He asks, "Did you finish the chair?" The man answers, "No."
10. The supervisor is angry. He asks, "Why didn't you finish?" The man says, "I can't find a screwdriver."

Expansion Exercises

Discussion: See Exercise H for discussion questions.

Imperatives—Following Directions: Give the students two-, three- or multiple-step directions to follow in completing a task. For example, "Open the door. Close the window. Put the book on the desk." Add negative commands. For example, "Don't stand up."

Imperatives—Building a Structure: Have the students form two groups and go to opposite ends of the room. If possible create a partition between them. Have the students in one group build a structure with blocks, rods, or other objects. Then have the first group instruct the students in the other group how to make an identical structure without looking at the structure. For example, "Put the red block on the round blue block." Students then compare structures.

Sequencing: Give students individual cards with illustrated directions for completing a task. Have students put the directions in order.

Matching: Give students individual cards with written directions for completing a task. Have students match the written cards to cards with illustrated directions.

Expressing Need: Give each student all of the items necessary for completing a task except for one important item. Give the students a short period of time for completing the task. Offer assistance to those students who express a need for the missing item.

Map: The story takes place at the ABA Factory. Have students locate the factory on the map. (See map on inside front cover.)

B. Number the pictures in order.
Answers: First column: 9, 5, 6, 4, 3. Second column: 1, 8, 7, 10, 2.

C. Match the picture with the sentence.
Answers: 1. c 2. g 3. e 4. a 5. b 6. d 7. f

D. Listen to the teacher.
The teacher reads a sentence from the script. The students circle the clock which shows the time they hear. Then they write the time in numerals on the blank line.
Script:

1. Finish this by 10:05.
2. See you at 2:30.
3. Come back to work at 2:45.
4. I start work at 6:15 in the morning.
5. I leave for work at 5:05 everyday.
6. Call me back at 12:55.
7. Our afternoon break begins at 2:10.
8. I take a break at 10:25.

Answers: 1. b 2. a 3. b 4. b 5. b 6. c 7. c 8. a

Expansion Exercises

Telling Time: "It's _____o'clock;...half past _____;... quarter to/of_____;..._____thirty; A.M and P.M." Use a clock with movable hands or give pairs of students small clock faces. Call out a time and have the students take turns setting the large clock, or their individual clocks in pairs, to the time you say.

Asking for Information: Teach/review ways to ask for clarification. For example, "Please repeat. I didn't understand.

What time? 10:00 or 11:00?" Read the script above very quickly or with unclear pronunciation. Wait for students to ask for clarification.

E. Three in a Row
Have students play the game. (See Introduction, Play the Game, page ix.)

F. True or False
Answers: 1. T 2. F 3. F 4. F 5. T 6. T 7. T

G. Fill in the blanks.
Answers: 1. chair 2. box 3. pieces 4. screwdriver 5. 2:00 6. supervisor 7. chair 8. says 9. angry 10. find

H. What do you think?
Students may want to discuss:

- how to communicate with one's boss.

- employer's expectations.

- appropriate ways of reporting problems in the workplace.

UNIT 12   PACKING   Page 67

Topic
Packing for Different Purposes

Functions
Making choices; expressing preferences.

Situation
A man is packing to go to college.

Cultural Notes
In the U.S., people may attend colleges far away from their homes. Some people live with friends or alone off campus. Others live in campus residences.

Some newcomers may experience difficulties selecting clothing for specific purposes or conditions (for example, a job interview, different weather conditions).

Grammar Focus
Nouns; Articles; *Going to* + Infinitive

Exercises

A. Talk about the pictures.

1. A man gets a letter. He can go to Y.U. College.
2. He puts a suitcase on the bed.
3. He puts a pair of pants in the suitcase. He's going to pack a pair of sunglasses.
4. He puts the pair of sunglasses in the suitcase. He's going to pack a pair of shoes.
5. He puts the pair of shoes in the suitcase. He's going to pack a pair of socks.
6. He puts the pair of socks in the suitcase. He's going to pack a pair of gloves.
7. He puts the pair of gloves in the suitcase. He's going to pack a pair of underwear.
8. He puts the pair of underwear in the suitcase. He's going to pack a dog.
9. He puts the dog in the suitcase.
10. He thinks about what (else) to pack.

Expansion Exercises

Discussion: See Exercise H for discussion questions.

Clothing: Bring in a variety of clothing items. Teach/review the names of the items. Have students separate the items according to gender, age, appropriateness for particular jobs, or appropriateness for particular weather conditions. Have the students talk about when various clothing items should be used.

Personal Items: Give students a variety of pictures of personal items. Have students decide which items would be appropriate for different kinds of trips (for example, an overnight trip, a camping trip, a trip to another country).

Nouns: Have students suggest other items commonly referred to as "a pair of." For example, mittens, pajamas, stockings, scissors, earrings.

Articles: More advanced students can practice changing *a/an* to *the* when a reference has been previously made to an object (as shown in the script above).

Gong to + *Infinitive:* Practice this structure with the picture story phrases, then ask students, "What are you going to do after class; work; this weekend?"

Map: This man lives in another town. He is going to live on campus at Y.U. College. Have students locate the campus on the map. (See map on inside front cover.)

B. Number the pictures in order.
Answers: First column: 9, 4, 1, 2, 5.   Second column: 6, 10, 8, 3, 7.

C. Match the picture with the sentence.
Answers: 1. c 2. d 3. g 4. a 5. b 6. f 7. e

D. Vocabulary—Circle the words.
Teach the names of the items listed by showing pictures of the objects or by showing the actual items. Put all of the pictures or items on a table. Call out the names of the items. Ask individual students to locate the items.

E. The Packing Game
Have students play the game. (See Introduction, Play the Game, page ix.)

Expansion Exercises

Packing Relay: Put duplicate clothing item types in two large boxes in the front of the room. Divide the class into two teams and have each team line up for a relay race. Call out the name of an item of clothing. The first person on each team goes to his/her team's box, finds and puts on the item. A point is given to the first student who puts on the item. Continue until all the students have a turn.

Packing Words: Put a suitcase or bag on a desk or counter. Write the names of clothing items on cards and put them on another desk or counter. Select one student to be the "packer." Give the other students pictures of common clothing items. In turn, students look at their pictures and tell the student who is packing what to pack. The student finds the correct written word and puts it in the suitcase. When the exercise has been completed, the students check the written words and the clothing pictures to find out if the correct words were chosen.

F. True or False
Answers: 1. T 2. F 3. T 4. F 5. T 6. T 7. F

G. Fill in the blanks.
Answers: 1. bedroom 2. suitcase 3. bed 4. pants 5. pair 6. packs 7. socks 8. gloves 9. underwear 10. dog

H. What do you think?

Students may want to discuss:

- College life in the U.S.
- Clothing worn for specific purposes (weather, jobs, sports, etc.).

UNIT 13   PANCAKES   Page 73

Topic
Following a Recipe

Functions
Apologizing; expressing satisfaction; giving and accepting compliments; making excuses; refusing an offer of food/drink.

Situation
A woman reads a recipe in order to make pancakes for a friend, but she makes mistakes following the recipe. Her friend says the pancakes are good but feeds them to the dog.

Cultural Notes
People cooking at home often follow recipes when preparing dishes that are new to them. People working in restaurants are often required to follow recipes listing exact measurements. Anyone following a recipe needs to be able to read basic vocabulary as well as measurements for volume and weight. The friend in this story acts inappropriately by giving the food to the dog. In the U.S., you can usually refuse the offer of food or drink if you do so politely and give a reason. (For example, "I just ate. Thanks but I'm on a diet. This tastes delicious but I'm so full.")

Grammar Focus
Imperatives; Present Continuous Tense; Count/Mass Nouns; Modals

Exercises

A. Talk about the pictures.

1. A woman wants to make pancakes. She reads a recipe. She reads "2 CUPS FLOUR."
2. The woman puts two cups of flour in the bowl.
3. She reads, "1 TSP SUGAR."
4. She puts one cup of sugar in the bowl.
5. She reads, "1 CUP MILK."
6. She puts one cup of milk in the bowl.
7. She reads, "MIX. FRY."
8. She puts the bowl in the oven. (She bakes the pancakes in the oven.)
9. She sits at the table with her friend. Her friend says, "They're good." (Her friend gives the pancakes to the dog.)

Expansion Exercises

Discussion: See Exercise H for discussion questions.

Imperatives: Bring in the ingredients for making a simple common dish. The teacher or an advanced student instructs students how to make the dish.

Present Continuous Tense: Give a cooking demonstration similar to a cooking show on TV (e.g., Julia Child) and describe to the audience what you are doing. Then have students practice giving cooking demonstrations for their classmates.

Recipe: Bring in the ingredients for making a simple common dish and a written recipe. The students read the recipe and make the dish. To practice asking for additional information and distinguishing count and mass nouns, the teacher can read the recipe aloud omitting the quantities. For example, "Add oil/eggs." Students then must ask, "How much?" or "How many?" questions to find out the quantity required.

Role-Play: Have students practice accepting and refusing food politely. Teach/review modals used for polite offers: "Would you like _____?" and appropriate responses. For example, "Thanks. I'd love some. Not now thanks. I've just eaten."

Map: The woman making the pancakes lives at 17 A Street. Her guest lives at 26 1st Street. Have the students trace/describe the route the guest took from 1st Street to A Street. (See map on inside front cover.)

B. Number the pictures in order.
Answers: First column: 8, 9, 7, 1, 2.   Second column: 3, 6, 5, 4.

C. Match the picture with the sentence.
Answers: 1. c 2. e 3. d 4. g 5. a 6. b 7. f

D. Vocabulary—Circle the words.
Teach the amounts and ingredients by showing pictures or by showing the actual items. Put all the ingredients and the measuring items on the table. Call out an ingredient and the amount to be measured. Ask the students to measure the amounts.

E. The Ingredients Game
Have students play the game. (See Introduction, Play the Game, page ix.)

Expansion Exercises

Count/Mass Nouns: Bring in pictures of food items and have students identify them. Then have the students divide the food items into count and mass nouns. Point out that adding a measurement word makes the item countable. For example, some oil versus 3 tbsp. oil; coffee versus a cup of coffee.

Matching: Prepare pictures of various measurements (e.g., 2 TBSP, 1 CUP, 3 TSP) on cards. Prepare another set of cards with the written measurements. Place the cards face down. Have students take turns turning over two cards at a time to try and make a match.

F. True or False
Answers: 1. T 2. F 3. F 4. F 5. T 6. F 7. T

G. Fill in the blanks.
Answers: 1. recipe 2. CUPS 3. flour 4. SUGAR 5. puts 6. bowl 7. pancakes 8. oven 9. gives 10. dog

H. What do you think?
Students may want to discuss:

- common American table manners.
- entertaining a guest including greetings, leave taking, offers of food.
- American food preferences.
- how to refuse an offer of food politely.

UNIT 14 STAY FOR DINNER Page 79

Topic
Parent/Child Relationships; Dating

Functions
Accepting/refusing invitations; expressing displeasure; expressing emotions; extending invitations; greeting/leave taking.

Situation
A girl's boyfriend shows up unexpectedly at her home and she invites him to stay for dinner. When the couple kiss at the end of the evening, the parents are angry.

Cultural Notes
In many cultures, the parents determine when a child is ready to have a relationship with someone of the opposite sex and who is acceptable. In the U.S., a teenager may form a serious relationship at school or at work that is not approved by the parents.

Grammar Focus
Past Tense; Pronouns; Possessive Adjectives

Exercises

A. Talk about the pictures.

1. A couple is sitting on a couch. A young man knocks at the door.
2. The man opens the door. The man asks, "Can I help you?" The visitor asks, "Is May here?"
3. The man calls his daughter. His daughter is thinking about Ed.
4. May asks, "What is it?" Her father says, "Ed's here."
5. May runs downstairs. Ed and May are glad to see each other.
6. Ed and May hug each other. Her parents watch them. (They're surprised.)
7. May asks, "Do you want to stay for dinner?" Ed says, "OK."
8. They eat dinner with May's parents.
9. Ed says, "Bye." Ed and May go outside.
10. Ed and May kiss. May's parents see them. They're angry.

Expansion Exercises

Discussion: See Exercise H for discussion questions.

Past Tense: Have students practice telling the story from the point of view of May, Ed, or the parents. Each person can tell it from his/her perspective as they would relate the incident to a friend after it happened.

Map: The story takes place at 4 Apple Road. Ask students to locate it on the map. The young man lives at 11 Post Office Road. Have students trace/describe the shortest route between the two places. (See map on inside front cover.)

B. Number the pictures in order.
Answers: First column: 2, 5, 4, 7, 6.   Second column: 9, 8, 1, 10, 3.

C. Match the picture with the sentence.
Answers: 1. e 2. f 3. g 4. a 5. c 6. d 7. b

D. Crossword Puzzle
Teach the relationship words by providing pictures of a family with the relationships labeled. Have students draw their own family trees with the names of family members and their relationships. Then have the students complete the exercise. The first letter of each relationship word is written in the crossword puzzle.

E. Listen to the teacher.
Teach days, times, and addresses. Put up a calendar in the classroom or write the days of the week on the board. Call out a day and have students point to that day. Write digital times on the board including A.M. and P.M. Read a time and have individual students point to the time read. Write several addresses on the board or show pictures of various places in town with house/building numbers. Call out the address of a place and ask individual students to point to that word or picture. Then read the script below and have students circle the information they hear. Remind students that they do not need to understand every word.

Script:

1. Ed, would you like to have dinner with my family on Thursday at 7:30 P.M.? Meet us at the coffee shop at 30 1st Street.
2. May , would you like to go to the baseball game with me on Saturday at 8:00 P.M.? The stadium in at 7 2nd street.
3. Hello. This is Dr. Brown's office. You have an appointment on Wednesday at 10:30 A.M. Our office is at 14 5th Street.
4. Hello, Mr. Lee. This is Mr. Smith. I'd like to meet with you on Friday at 3:00 P.M. My office is at 50 3rd Street.
5. Let's go to dinner this week. Can you meet me at the restaurant at 2 1st Street at 7:00 P.M. this Saturday?

Answers: 1. c, a, b 2. c, c, a 3. a, a, b 4. a, b, c 5. b, c, a

F. True or False
Answers: 1. T 2. F 3. F 4. T 5. F 6. T 7. F

G. Fill in the blanks.
Answers: 1. father 2. downstairs 3. other 4. mother 5. want 6. dinner 7. Bye 8. go 9. kiss 10. angry

Expansion Exercise

Pronouns and Possessive Adjectives: Have students rewrite the account of the pictures in Exercise A, changing all the nouns to pronouns (for example, *May* to *she*) and the possessive nouns to possessive adjectives (*May's* to *her*).

H. What do you think?
Students may want to discuss:

- dating in the U.S.
- the role of parents in dating.
- the expectations of parents and children in the dating ritual.

UNIT 15 THE TOASTER Page 85

Topic
Household Safety

Functions
Expressing anger; expressing pain.

Situation
A man puts bread in a toaster. One piece of toast pops up but the other does not. He puts a knife in the toaster and gets a shock.

Cultural Notes

People new to the U.S. may not be aware that metal objects (e.g., knives, forks) should *never* be put inside a toaster unless it is unplugged. It is easy to receive an electrical shock or even be killed. Electrical appliances such as toasters and sharp metal objects should be kept out of the reach of children.

Grammar Focus

Imperatives; Prepositions of Place; Nouns: Container Words; Ordinal Numbers

Exercises

A. Talk about the pictures.

1. The man puts two pieces of bread in the toaster.
2. He puts away the loaf of bread. (He puts the loaf of bread on the shelf.)
3. He pushes down the lever (bar, button).
4. He waits for the toast to come up.
5. The first piece of toast pops up/comes up. He says, "One."
6. The other piece of toast doesn't pop up/come up. He asks, "Where is the second piece of toast?"
7. He looks in the toaster.
8. He puts a knife in the toaster.
9. He gets a shock.

Expansion Exercises

Discussion: See Exercise H for discussion questions.

Imperatives: Bring in real electrical appliances or equipment or pictures of items (for example, a tape recorder, a blender, a toaster, a radio) and have the students practice giving and responding to commands to make the appliance function. For example, "Push the button." Variation: *Simon Says.*

Nouns—Container Words: Bring in food items (or pictures) and have students identify them. Then have students describe the packaging for these food items (for example, a loaf of bread, a box of cookies, a jar of jam).

Role-Play: Have students role-play the sequence of events in the story.

Map: This story takes place at 23 Apple Road. Have students locate the house on the map. (See map on inside front cover.)

B. Number the pictures in order.

Answers: First column: 7, 9, 2, 1, 8.   Second column: 6, 5, 4, 3.

C. Match the picture with the sentence.

Answers: 1. c 2. d 3. f 4. a 5. b 6. g 7. e

D. Listen to the teacher.

Draw shelves on the board labeled with ordinal numbers 1st though 5th. Read a number and have students point to the one you read.
Script:

1. Put the salt on the bottom shelf.
2. The juice is on the middle shelf.
3. Put away the soup on the top shelf.
4. I put the rice on the shelf above the juice.
5. I think the bread is on the shelf below the juice.

Answers: 1. 5th 2. 3rd 3. 1st 4. 2nd 5. 4th

Expansion Exercises

Storage: Give students an assortment of safe and potentially unsafe items (for example, soap, oven cleaner, a knife). Provide pictures of common storage spaces (for example, cupboard, drawer, shelf, refrigerator, closet) and have students put the items next to the appropriate card.

Prepositions of Place: Have the students practice using *in* and *on* by having them tell where to put different items. They can practice other prepositions of place by following and giving directions to place items in different areas of the classroom.

Numbers: Write ordinal and cardinal numbers 1 through 10 on the board in random order. Call out an ordinal number. Have students take turns going to the board, finding and circling the numbers they hear. Then ask the students to give the equivalent cardinal number. Make this activity into a game with teams.

E. Match the picture with the number and the word.
Answers: 1. c, h 2. b, f 3. d, j 4. a, g 5. e, i

F. True or False
Answers: 1. T 2. F 3. F 4. T 5. T 6. F 7. F

G. Fill in the blanks.
Answers: 1. toaster 2. piece 3. bread 4. shelf 5. waits 6. comes 7. second 8. toast 9. picks 10. knife

H. What do you think?
Students may want to discuss:

- potential problems with appliances in the home.
- coping with medical emergencies.

UNIT 16   THE WALLET   Page 91

Topic
Safety in the City; Legal Rights and Responsibilities; Honesty

Functions
Expressing ambivalence; expressing need; expressing want or desire; making decisions; questioning values.

Situation
A woman finds a wallet on the street and thinks about using the money to buy things she wants but can't afford. She has to decide whether to buy shoes or give the wallet to the police.

Cultural Notes
Carrying proper identification in a wallet or purse enables whoever finds it if lost to return it to the owner or give it to the police. In many cultures, people living in rural areas or in small towns—even those who are poor—feel an obligation to return a lost item to its owner. People know and naturally provide support for others in small communities. In urban areas in the U.S., people do not know each other as well and often live in isolation. Urban poverty can provide an additional challenge to people maintaining their traditional beliefs and attitudes.

Grammar Focus
WH Questions; Past and Present Continuous Tenses; Prepositions

Exercises

A. Talk about the pictures.

1. A man is at a bus stop. He's going to get on a bus.
2. He gets on the bus. His wallet falls out of his pocket.
3. A woman walks to the bus stop. Her shoes are old (worn).
4. She sees the wallet on the sidewalk.
5. She finds money and an ID in the wallet.
6. She thinks about clothes (a coat, a dress) she can buy with the money.
7. She sees a shoe store across the street.
8. She thinks about buying a new pair of shoes.
9. She sees a police station.
10. She thinks about what to do.

Expansion Exercises

Discussion: See Exercise G for discussion questions.

Role-Play: Divide students into small groups and have each group develop an ending to this story. Have the groups role-play their endings. Then discuss any differences in the endings that the students create.

WH Questions: Have students ask each other WH questions about each of the frames. For example, "What falls out of the man's pocket? Where is the shoe store? What does the woman think about buying?"

Past and Present Continuous: Have students tell the story in the past as if they are the woman who found the wallet and she is describing to a friend what happened.

Prioritizing: Give students a list or pictures of items (for example, a TV, children's clothing, toys, etc). Have students work individually or in groups to number the items according to their importance to them. Students share their lists and give reasons for their choices.

Map: This event takes place in front of the police station on California Street. The shoe store the woman sees is across the street. Have students locate the two places on the map. (See map on inside front cover.)

B. Number the pictures in order.
Answers: First column: 9, 3, 8, 4, 6.   Second column: 1, 10, 5, 2, 7.

C. Match the picture with the sentence.
Answers: 1. b 2. e 3. f 4. d 5. a 6. g 7. c

D. The Map Game
Teach the place names by showing pictures of actual places in the community or by showing items found at each place. Mark off the classroom floor into streets. Label streets and places according to the map grid in the Map Game. Call out a street or place name, for example, the clinic. Ask indi-vidual students to go to the place you call out. Ask students to find a place and tell where it is located. For example, Teacher: "Where's the bus station?" Student: "On C Street." Have students play the game. (See Introduction, Play the Game, page ix.)

Expansion Exercises

Prepositions: Draw a simple map grid on the board to indicate streets horizontally and vertically. Write common community place names on the map. Call out the name of a place. Ask students to point to the place you call out and then to identify places on the map which are behind, across from, beside, or near each place you name.

Listening: Have the students look at the first map. Read the script below and have the students listen and write the sentence number in the appropriate place on the map. Script:

Number 1. I need to see the doctor at the *clinic.*
Number 2. Ted said, "Take *bus number 8.*"
Number 3. I think the *bank* is closed today.
Number 4. Please think about going to the *police station.*
Number 5. I think she lives on *C Street.*

The Community: Put common names for places in the community (e.g., bank, post office, supermarket) randomly up on the board. Divide the class into two teams. Read one of the place names aloud. One student from each team runs to the board and touches the correct place name. The first one to touch it wins. OR Hold up a picture or symbol that corresponds to the place name and have students find the name on the board.

Matching: Prepare cards with common community place names written on them. For example, bookstore, gas station, hospital. Also prepare cards illustrating the meaning of each community place. Place the cards face down. Have students take turns turning over two cards at a time to try and make a match.

E. True or False
Answers: 1. T 2. F 3. T 4. T 5. T 6. F 7. F

F. Fill in the blanks.
Answers: 1. bus 2. wallet 3. woman 4. ID 5. dress 6. store 7. shoes 8. police 9. thinks 10. money

G. What do you think?
Students may want to discuss:

- how people cope with pressures of poverty.
- attitudes toward the police.
- the needs of people new to the U.S.
- conflict between traditional values and those that exist in some urban poverty-stricken areas.

Acknowledgments

The authors are very grateful to our friends and colleagues in the U.S. Department of State, Bureau for Refugee Affairs, Refugee Education and Training Programs who have given their support and shared their ideas, and to the refugees who tried out our activities while preparing for U.S. resettlement in the refugee camps in Thailand, Indonesia, the Philippines, the Sudan, and Eastern Europe. We also appreciate the comments and suggestions from teachers who have used *Picture Stories* with their classes and from faculty and students at the School for International Training, Brattleboro, Vermont, who have tried out activities in *Picture Stories* as part of the MAT training program.

Special thanks go to: the original group of administrators, supervisors, and teachers on Galang; Lois Purdham and Joanne Dresner who first encouraged us to publish these stories; Lynn Savage for her invaluable advice on the manuscript from beginning to end; Janet Isserlie for her helpful comments as we made our final changes; Vichuda Lungtaisong, Andrea Murphy, Fran Covey, Rochelle Clark, Michael Silberman, and Lynn Lederer for their logistical support, friendship and sense of humor; Claude Pepin, Don Batchelder, Helju Batchelder, Al Hoel and David Belskis for making both volumes of *Picture Stories* possible; at Longman, Debbie Sistino for her many hours of advice, assistance, patience and good humor and Andrea West and Richard Bretan for putting the pieces together; and to Jim, Jonathan, and Elizabeth Rodgers; Peter, Marcus and Andrew Falion; and George Tannenbaum for their patience, support and understanding.